CENTRAL ITALY

Vernon Bartlett

CENTRAL ITALY

B. T. Batsford Ltd, London

First published 1972
© Vernon Bartlett 1972.

Text printed in Great Britain by Northumberland Press Ltd,
Gateshead. Plates printed and books bound by Richard Clay
(The Chaucer Press) Ltd, Bungay, Suffolk

ISBN 0 7134 0164 8

Contents

Foreword

I have not compiled a bibliography: a list of books, articles and so on from which I have had to supplement my own knowledge would be too long. But I must express my gratitude to some individuals who have given me advice and help. Dr Alberto Droandi, Director of the *Ente Provinciale per il Turismo* in Arezzo, and Mr John Greenwood, of the Italian State Tourist Office in London, have supplemented their official advice by their valued personal friendship. Dr Giuseppe Agozzino, Director of the *Azienda Autonoma per il Turismo* in Perugia, was very helpful and hospitable at a time when he was in great pain, resulting from an accident. Dr Soldoni, Director of the Azienda Autonoma in Spoleto, enabled me to see a lot in the rather short time I could spend in that attractive city. And then there are friends whose sole reason for helping me is their friendship – Dr Michael Grant, the most industrious author I have ever met, who nevertheless found time to read several chapters (although he has, of course, no responsibility for any errors that may remain); Professor Luigi Biagi and Signora Elle Milani, who have had the patience to read, and to comment upon, the whole book; and Mr Rex Probert, of London, who, in his brief and busy visits to Italy, has acquired such a knowledge of the country. My thanks to them all.

I add a paragraph about the use of the word 'condottiere'. In a recent book, I used the word *'condottiero'*, and was reproached for so doing by several readers, including one of Britain's most famous literary critics. But the Italians themselves say *'condottiero'*, which Webster's Dictionary claims is erroneous. It obviously is not erroneous in Italian. Hence a small dilemma. But fortunately most dictionaries use 'condottiere' as an English word, with 'condottieri' as the plural. So will Italian readers please note that, when I write 'condottiere', I am writing English and not bad Italian, and that I am still writing English when I use 'condottieri' to denote more than one of these leaders of mercenary troops.

Acknowledgments

The Publishers wish to thank the following for supplying photographs reproduced in the book : J. Allan Cash for plates 1, 9 and 21; Foto-Enit-Roma for plate 22; and A. F. Kersting for plates 2-7, 10-13, 15-17, 19 and 23-25.

The Plates

1. Introduction and a little History

No other country – not even Greece or Persia or China – has contributed so much and over so long a period as Italy to our civilisation. We still put up buildings copied from those of the Ancient Romans. For centuries, the intellectual and social life of Europe depended upon the Popes and the men upon whom they conferred the crown of the Holy Roman Empire. In the thirteenth and fourteenth centuries, Venice was the most important channel through which the exports of the Indies and the Far East reached Western Europe. Florence was the birthplace of the Renaissance, and the courts of Milan, Ferrara, Urbino and other Northern Italian cities attracted artists and intellectuals from every part of the known world. Five or six centuries ago, the universities of Bologna, Padua and other cities were attended by students from all over Europe.

And yet one fact – a fact that goes far to explain the politics of Italy today – is almost always overlooked. This old country is relatively new. It was only in 1860 that Garibaldi, Mazzini and Cavour were able to create an Italian nation. Even then, unity was incomplete, for the Pope refused to accept this unity under an Italian king; it was not until 1870 that Italian troops broke through the walls of Rome, and the papal territorial possessions, still covering an important area in the centre of the country, were reduced to the 100-odd acres of the Vatican City. Not surprisingly, patriotism has been regional rather than national, and even today a man is more likely to boast that he is a Pisan, a Neapolitan or a Venetian than that he is an Italian.

This is still a great political handicap for Italy, but it does also mean that the country has retained a splendid variety of local customs and loyalties that adds enormously to its fascination for the foreign visitor. It is mainly for visitors who are interested in this variety that this book is written. It is NOT a guide book. It will NOT be of much use to those tourists who 'do' Florence or Ravenna in a day and want to be sure they have seen – or at least glanced at – all the right pictures and been in all the right churches. Its aim is more modest – to call the reader's attention to some of the places and events that have increased the author's affectionate interest in this land of his adoption.

Also I must at once explain what area I have included under the title, *Central Italy*, and why I have done so. In the south, I have omitted Rome because, had I included it, there would be so little space for anything else. (My Baedeker on *Central Italy* devotes 280 pages of text to Rome, with another 73 pages to its environs, out of a total of 504 pages.) So I have not gone south of a line running roughly from Civitavecchia, on the west coast, through Viterbo, to Ascoli Piceno, near the east coast. On the other hand, I have penetrated farther north than did Baedeker and several other guides to Central Italy, in order to follow very roughly the old Roman frontier between Italy and Cisalpine Gaul. That is to say, my frontier runs from the mouth of the Magra River a few miles south of La Spezia, on the west, along the mountains just north of Lucca, Pistoia and Florence, and thence to Ravenna, on the east coast. Ravenna, it is true, was a few miles inside Cisalpine Gaul, but it is more easily visited by people from Rimini and other Adriatic resorts than from Venice, Verona, Parma, Padua or other towns on the great plain of the River Po. Besides, how could I omit a city that was for centuries the political capital of Italy ... and that has all those mosaics?

*   *   *

Why do more than 20 million people visit Italy every year? One can, to a great extent, sort out their reasons in terms of geography. Most of the visitors one meets in the wide valley of the River Po are likely to be interested in history and archi- tecture, for without that interest the hot, flat plain would soon become monotonous. Those who visit Tuscany and Umbria come for the pictures, the architecture but also for the moun- tain scenery – there must be scores of books about the hill-towns of Central Italy. Those who crowd into the hotels and camping sites along the coast come to swim, to lie in deck chairs, to drink their Campari or their Punt e Mes on café terraces. But even these escapists from cold northern climes might find that some knowledge of history could add to the pleasure of their holiday. The Cathedral in Florence becomes more interesting if one knows of the attempt by members of a rival banking family to murder Lorenzo the Magnificent and his brother during High Mass. One likes to be shown the lamp in Pisa cathedral, the swinging of which led Galileo to one of his greatest discoveries, even though the particular lamp was not there when Galileo was alive. One may go to Monza for the motor races, but one may also see there the Iron Crown which was used at the coronation of Charlemagne on Christmas Day, 800, and subsequently at those of many other emperors of the Holy Roman Empire. I imagine that in no other country does some knowledge of his- tory add so much to one's enjoyment.

So the rest of this section is an attempt to give some kind of historical background to your holiday in Central Italy. It can be omitted by the tourist in a hurry, but I hope it won't be.

Legend merges into history with the alleged foundation of Rome in 753 B.C. by Romulus and Remus, the twin grand- children of the ruler of a small kingdom in the Alban Hills, now so favourite a region for Roman holiday-makers. An ambitious great-uncle may, in actual fact, have ordered that they should be drowned in the Tiber, but at that point legend again inter- venes by stopping the flow of the river and by providing a she-wolf to suckle the infants until a shepherd found them and gave them a more normal upbringing. Their ancestors had crossed the Alps and migrated down the peninsula nearly 1,000 years earlier with several other tribes, and had settled in the mountains on either side of the Tiber.

By the time they began to build Rome, Greeks and Phoenicians were already colonising southern Italy and Sicily, and the Etruscans had spread over most of the land we now call Tuscany. These Etruscans supplied some of Rome's earlier kings, and their knowledge of working in metals, based mainly on their use of the iron ore on the island of Elba, certainly had a great deal to do with the growth of Rome, established at a point where a small island, the Isola Tiberina, made the river crossing relatively easy. At a very early date, the Etruscans were exporting iron to Greece and the Eastern Mediterranean in exchange for gold and other precious metals, which they worked with very great skill. After the Roman conquest of Etruria, most of these metals were sent overland, by way of Rome, down to the heel of Italy to shorten the sea voyage, with its dangers from storms and pirates, and one may presume that the Romans exacted heavy duties on this traffic.

Who were these Etruscans? With the Basques, the Finns and the Hungarians they remain one of the problem peoples of Europe, and their language, in structure and vocabulary, is unlike any of the Indo-European languages, although their alphabet was very close to that of Greece. As with Semitic, early Greek and early Latin writing, it was generally written from right to left, but it was sometimes in *boustrophedon* style, which means that one line was from right to left and the next from left to right – a system that lessened the reader's danger of skipping a line but must singularly have complicated the job for the writer. Visitors to the Villa Giulia museum in Rome or the Archaeological Museum in Florence, to say nothing of the smaller, local museums at Volterra, Chiusi, Tarquinia and others of the original 12 cities of the Etruscan Federation will at once notice how strongly this people was influenced by Greek ideas

2   *Lucca: the cathedral*

and mythology. But they will also notice very significant differences. There is much more vitality and realism in their paintings than in Greek paintings of the same period – indeed, some experts find nothing to compare with them until after Giotto had prepared the way for the Renaissance, some 2,000 years later. Somewhere about 400 B.C. – possibly resulting from their conquest by the Romans – their paintings of banquets and dances changed, and began to reveal a frightened preoccupation with death and the possible horrors of after-life. It is from the Etruscans that the Western world inherited horned demons hurrying unfortunates along the road to Hell with spiked tridents. The Greeks portrayed Charon as an ugly, grubby old man, exacting his toll from every passenger he rowed across the Styx: the Etruscans made him even uglier and more malevolent, carrying a double-headed hammer in his hand, with which he could give his passengers the *coup-de-grâce*, and they pictured him with a particularly hideous demon, known as Tuchulcha, as his attendant.

But who were these Etruscans? The Latins, to the south of them, the Umbrians to the east, and the Ligurians, to the north, had trekked down from the Alps, and some historians claim either that the Etruscans followed the same route or that they were the original inhabitants of central Italy, established there before the great waves of migration across eastern Europe from central Asia. I would rather believe those other historians who claim that, like the Greeks and the Phoenicians, these particular migrants came by sea. Certainly, both as enemies and as allies of the Phoenicians, they showed all the qualities of a seafaring people. And one has the authority of Herodotus, 'the father of history' (who himself migrated from Greece to southern Italy in the fifth century B.C.) for the story that they came from Lydia, in Asia Minor, as the result of nearly two decades of famine, during which their king allowed them to eat only on alternate days. On fasting days, in order to take their minds off their hunger, he made them play all kinds of games, most of which they invented as they went along. (Among their inven-

3 *Lucca: the Roman amphitheatre, now a vegetable market*

tions were real coinage and the dice which have been responsible in the course of history for the transfer of so many coins
from one gambler to another.) The games, however, did not
abolish the famine. The king and his son, Tyrrhenos, decided
that half the tribe must emigrate, and the son led a fleet in
which, to quote Herodotus, 'they came to the land of the Umbrians, and there they established towns in which they live to
this day. But they gave up the name of Lydians and took the
name of the king's son who had led them, calling themselves
Tyrrhenians'. (The sea which washes the shores of western
Italy – rather ineffectually, since the Mediterranean has so little
tide – is still called the Tyrrhenian Sea.)

Among the very many reasons – too many to be mentioned
here – for the belief that Herodotus was right, is most unexpectedly, a bronze model of a sheep's liver with Etruscan letters
scratched on it, which was found at Piacenza, in northern Italy.
This was undoubtedly used by the Etruscan *haruspices*, whose
job it was to foretell the future by studying entrails, and
especially livers, of men and beasts, and it is significant that
several terracotta models of livers have been found in Asia
Minor, especially near Babylon.

In all probability then, the Etruscans did come originally from
Asia Minor, but it is obvious that the number of men who
could have been carried by even a large fleet of such small ships
could not have been sufficient to enable them to occupy almost
the whole of central Italy, already populated by Umbrians,
Sabines, Latins and other tribes. The first Etruscan settlers must
have been followed by others over several generations, and all
of them may have lived for some time in Lemnos or others of
the Greek islands on the way, absorbing Greek ideas while they
did so. But there were certainly enough of them to ensure
that their descendants, the Tuscans of today, have certain
characteristics that distinguish them from all the other peoples
who make up the very mixed population of Italy.

For some three centuries, these Etruscans were more important than the Romans themselves. I have already mentioned their influence in Rome where, amongst other things, their principal gods, Tinia, Uni and Menrva, became the Roman gods, Jupiter, Juno and Minerva. But for the purposes of this book, their importance lies in their spread northwards. Their advance up the west coast was checked, north of Pisa, by the Ligurians, firmly established along the shores of what is now the Italian Riviera. But they turned inland and, where Florence now stands, crossed the Apennines, over the passes which our cars had to follow until the tunnels and bridges of the *autostrada* from Florence to Bologna enabled them to pass through mountains and across deep valleys. Once over the mountains, the Etruscans had little difficulty in spreading out across the plain of the Po, to Milan and the foothills of the Alps in the north and to the east coast from Pesaro and Rimini very nearly to Venice. Thus, even as far north as Ferrara, there is a very good Etruscan museum.

Rome's last king, Tarquin the Proud, was an Etruscan. In 510 B.C. the Romans were said to have deposed him and sent him into exile. The Etruscans failed to reinstate him, for they had over-estimated their strength and the degree of unity between their cities. Later they suffered at the hands of 'barbarians' (Celtic-speaking Gauls) who had crossed the Alps and were establishing themselves on the plain of the Po, and who, in 390 or 387 B.C., marched south as far as Rome. These Gauls may have failed to capture the Capitol (thanks, if legend is to be believed, to the alarm given by the geese) but they sacked the rest of the city and withdrew only after the Romans had paid a very large ransom. On their way north again, they destroyed town after town; by the middle of the third century B.C., Etruria had passed into history, but meanwhile it had provided an opportunity for the Romans to build up their power. By 49 B.C., when Julius Caesar's dictatorship in effect put an end to the republican system which had been instituted after the overthrow of Tarquin, the Roman dominions spread all along the northern coast of the Mediterranean and included the valuable wheat-growing African province of Tunis, as well as the greater part of the Iberian peninsula.

Caesar expressed his decision by action. Six years earlier, in a meeting at Lucca, he, Pompey and Crassus, the three strongest men in Italy who formed what was known as the First Triumvirate, had agreed on their respective zones of influence for the next five years. Under this agreement, Caesar was to govern Gaul and what was known as Cisalpine Gaul (namely Italy between the Alps and a line running across the peninsula from a little to the north of present-day Viareggio on the west coast to the Adriatic a little to the north of Rimini). The frontier of his territory on the Adriatic side was marked by a miserable little stream called the Rubicon; south of the Rubicon, he must not go.

This agreement gave Caesar plenty of scope for military activity, but he was also interested in politics, especially after the death of Crassus had put too much power in the hands of Pompey, as ambitious as he was himself. His army had been very successful north of the Alps (except for two short-lived invasions of south-eastern England); its success south of the Rubicon would be still more useful to him. So, in January of 49 B.C., with two small but very mobile columns, he crossed this border stream. City after city opened its gates to him to avoid destruction. The Senate panicked, and fled from Rome. Pompey fled from Italy altogether – he went to Egypt where Ptolemy, who had promised him safe refuge, had him assassinated as soon as he landed. Caesar became dictator and, five years later, was himself assassinated at the foot of Pompey's statue.

Caesar did not call himself emperor. In the words of Shakespeare's Mark Antony, 'I thrice presented him a kingly crown, which he did thrice refuse'. But he had made himself 'perpetual dictator', which was much the same thing. Octavian, his great-nephew, who succeeded him after twenty years of disturbance and civil war, was at first very careful not to arouse the hostility of the Senate. He claimed that he was returning to the constitution of the Republic, but he took the pretentious title of Augustus and became the first of a long line of emperors, some good, some notoriously bad and some indifferent.

Despite the bad ones, the Empire held together for more than 300 years, until the accession of Constantine, remembered mainly as the first emperor to become a Christian, but also noteworthy because he split the Empire into two, with the headquarters of the Western Empire in Milan and, later, Ravenna, and those of the Eastern Empire in Constantinople, a new city built on the foundations of the old Greek city of Byzantium. He established himself in Constantinople, and Rome was thus robbed of its prestige and its defenders: in 378 began the barbaric invasions – first, the Visigoths from the Danubian plain, then the Vandals, from the Rhineland, and then, most feared of all, Attila and his Huns.

Attila, however, never got beyond Lake Garda, where he was stopped not by an army, but by Pope Leo I. For a strange development had taken place in Rome since the division of the empire into two. Power had passed from Roman patricians who, until Constantine, had treated Christians with open hostility or contemptuous tolerance, to the leaders of Christianity, the popes. Leo I travelled north and persuaded Attila to retire, and the fact that this great general died a few months later at the end of his wedding banquet was widely attributed to a miracle, and not – as it probably was – to an attack of apoplexy. Rome, as the headquarters of Christianity, a religion which had great and growing power throughout Europe, was acquiring an influence that was to predominate for well over 1,000 years.

There were, of course, the Western representatives of the Emperor in Constantinople, but they lived in Milan or Ravenna, and did little to help or to hinder the Popes in Rome. They were not even all Italians; one of the greatest of them, Odoacer (also known as Ottokar) was a German who had been a successful officer in the imperial army, and was proclaimed king by his troops with such vehemence that the Romans judged it wise to accept their proclamation. He emphasised his independence by sending back to the Eastern emperor the diadem and purple robes of the Western Empire with the remark that they would not be needed any more since the West could look after itself.

The Eastern emperor had other views. He encouraged the Ostrogoths to invade Italy in 489 and their leader, Theodoric, having invited Odoacer to dinner in Ravenna, cleft his skull in two. In the subsequent 33 years, he maintained power in part because he distributed one-third of all Italian territory amongst his soldiers, thus giving them an important vested interest in the *status quo*. (This was not an innovation; Caesar and other Roman generals had rewarded their troops in this way. But in Theodoric's case it was also an attempt to merge Romans and Goths into one people.)

After Theodoric's burial, in a famous round tomb in Ravenna, the Eastern emperor, Justinian, took still more active steps to bring this Western Empire back under his control. These steps were disastrous from Italy's point of view, but temporarily successful from his. Two excellent Byzantine generals, Belisarius and Narses, over-ran the country and re-established Ravenna as the Eastern Empire's headquarters in the west. Narses was 75 when he landed in Italy, and he remained as the Exarch, or emperor's representative, until he was well into his nineties. Italy regained her liberation from this Byzantine control only with the unexpected help of one more horde of invaders, this time the *Longobardi* or Lombards. They came to stay. With Pavia as their capital they occupied the rich plain of the Po and most of Tuscany. They also formed two separate duchies of Spoleto and Benevento, thereby limiting the power of the Eastern Empire in the south. For two centuries, Italy was ruled by the Lombards, but, under their rule, the popes were able to increase their influence while that of the Eastern emperors diminished.

The next development was the formation of what was known as the Holy Roman Empire. This came about after the Lombards had captured Ravenna, the stronghold of the Eastern Emperor in the west, in 751, which so alarmed the pope of that day that he appealed for help to yet another people from north of the Alps, the Franks. Their army drove the Lombards out of

4   *Lucca: the church of San Frediano*

Ravenna and their king, Pepin, sent the keys of that city, not back to the Eastern Emperor in Constantinople, but to the Pope in Rome. The breach between the Western and Eastern Empires was thus completed. On Christmas Day, 800, Pepin's son, Charlemagne, was crowned emperor by Pope Leo III in St Peter's. For a time, the alliance between these two men gave to the new Roman Empire an influence almost as great as it had been under Augustus and Trajan.

But the time was not very long. By replacing Ravenna and other cities under the direct rule of the pope, Pepin had sown the seeds which were bound to bring later popes into conflict with later emperors. The popes found it useful to have the support of the imperial armies and the emperors found it useful to claim that they had God on their side, but the latent rivalry between them has bedevilled Italian history for almost 1,000 years. Emperors wanted to unite Italy under their control; popes were against such union, since it would have robbed them of their temporal power, their rule over much of central Italy. It was that rivalry which led Pope Pius IX to oppose Garibaldi, Mazzini and Cavour when they tried to unite Italy in 1860, and one finds traces of it in Italian politics even today.

With absentee emperors (Charlemagne had been crowned in Rome but his headquarters were in Aachen, in north-west Germany) and popes with territorial ambitions, the whole country was divided against itself. The men appointed by the emperors were often foreigners and the local population often turned to the priests instead. Big landowners took the government into their own hands, and became very rich in the process. Some served the popes and some served the emperors, and many changed their loyalties when it paid them well to do so. They divided into Guelfs, who tended to support the popes, and Ghibellines, who tended to support the emperors – the names were taken from two rival families in southern Germany, and in their origin had nothing whatsoever to do with Italy. They hired mercenaries, known as *condottieri*, to fight their

5   *Pisa: columns supporting Giovanni Pisano's pulpit in the cathedral*

wars. They rivalled each other in their encouragement of artists and writers during that incredible period known as the Renaissance.

The Renaissance in the fourteenth to the sixteenth centuries was a period of intellectual and artistic greatness without rival in history. Giotto, who died in 1337, introduced a new realism into painting, as did Donatello and Jacopo della Quercia, born in the second half of that century, into sculpture. Brunelleschi, their contemporary, showed a miraculous understanding of engineering when he built the huge dome of Florence cathedral. They were followed, nearly a century later, by two artists, Leonardo da Vinci and Michelangelo, whose reputations stand above all others. But – since even artists cannot live only on bread and water – it has to be admitted that the flowering of genius in central and northern Italy might never have happened had there not been so much wealth, collected generally by the most brutal and ruthless methods, to give the artists status and encouragement.

This period of greatness was also one of the worst periods of civil strife. The ruined castles built on Tuscan hill-tops and surrounded by clusters of houses provide one of the greatest attractions of the landscape today, but they are also reminders of the senseless wars, based often on the rivalries and jealousies of the ducal families, that brought misery to the masses, and especially to those who worked on the land and who had no city walls within which they could find refuge.

The greatest of these ducal families was undoubtedly that of the Medici, who controlled Florence and a large part of Tuscany – roughly from the sea coast in the west to Arezzo and Cortona in the east – for most of the period between 1434 and 1494. Farther north, the Visconti and, later, the Sforza, based on Milan, ruled over a duchy that at one time included Genoa, Bologna, Verona and even Pisa and Siena. Other great families included the Scaligeri in Verona, the Gonzaga in Mantua and, inside the Papal States but paying little more than lip service to the popes, were the Este of Ferrara, the Montefeltro of

Urbino and the Malatesta of Rimini. All these small but wealthy states played their part in the intellectual flowering of the age, but also in civil wars that finally brought Italy under foreign rule from the sixteenth until the second half of the nineteenth century.

Southern Italy is outside the scope of this book but some mention must be made of its part in the history of the country as a whole. For a very brief period in the thirteenth century, it seemed possible that the Emperor Frederick II, an amazingly gifted man who lived in Sicily and was known as *Stupor Mundi*, the 'Wonder of the World', would succeed in creating an effective Roman Empire in Central Europe and a united Italian kingdom. But the popes were too strong. Frederick died in 1250, leaving little behind him beyond an unusual number of splendid castles. For reasons already mentioned, no pope wanted the unity of Italy, which could take place only at the expense of the Papal States; rather than recognise Manfred, one of Frederick's bastard sons, as emperor, the pope crowned Charles d'Anjou, brother of the King of France, as King of Sicily. This kingdom included not only the island of that name but also most of southern Italy, and in order to possess it Charles must first defeat Manfred. This he did. Manfred was killed in battle at Benevento and his step-brother, a boy of 16, was captured and publicly beheaded in Naples.

But there was still one survivor of Frederick Hohenstaufen's family – Manfred's daughter, Constance, who was married to a Spaniard, Peter, son of the King of Aragon. While the French Charles was trying to conquer the eastern end of Sicily, the Spanish Peter landed at the western end. Charles retired to Naples. He continued to call himself King of Sicily although he never managed to capture the island. From that time onwards, until after Garibaldi had landed in Sicily in 1860, Italy periodically became the battlefield between foreign kings.

Public opinion, of course, had very little influence in international affairs; nations became friends or enemies as best suited the ambitions of their rulers. Either by wars or by the judicious choice of husbands for their daughters, monarchs added large slabs of Europe to their existing kingdoms; the treaties that ended the Wars of the Spanish Succession, the Polish Succession and the Austrian Succession all made formidable changes to the maps of Italy. The rulers of the small states in the North paid heavily for their past squabbles by becoming, at best, puppets under the control of the French, the Spaniards or the Austrians, who governed in Milan or Florence until one ruling family with a reasonably good claim to be Italian – that of the House of Savoy – came out in defiance of the French and the Austrians and in support of Italian independence and of the efforts of Garibaldi, Cavour and Mazzini after the 1848 revolution in Paris had let loose a campaign throughout Europe against autocratic and despotic government.

Another twelve years passed before these three leaders of Italy's awakening nationalism – known as the *Risorgimento* – were successful and the head of the House of Savoy, Victor Emmanuel II, became king of all Italy apart from the Papal States, right in the centre. His capital was Florence (from 1865 to 1871), since the pope was still ruling in Rome. But ten years later, the outbreak of the Franco-Prussian war compelled Napoleon III to recall the French soldiers who were the principal defenders of the Papal States and Pope Pius IX had to surrender his temporal power, which he did with bad grace, ordering Italian Catholics to play no part in the politics of the new Italian nation.

This brief review of Italy's history may help one to understand the Italy of today. A contempt for the law and a cleverness in avoiding its more unpleasant aspects are much less signs of basic dishonesty than consequences of the fact that the rulers who imposed laws in the past were so often hated foreigners. The Italians had lived under so many different and rival regimes and therefore inherited different traditions and methods of government. The civil service is badly paid and incompetent but, still more, it is snowed under an unbelievable mass of administrative orders, many of them contradictory. And this breakdown of the bureaucracy, with its resultant delays in the payment of social benefits and so on, is one of the principal causes of the many strikes and instances of labour unrest, despite a remarkable increase of national wealth.

Again, the fact that the popes have played so dominating a part in politics for some 15 centuries leads to a very considerable intervention by the Vatican in national politics even today, and this, in turn, explains in part why Italy, despite its increasing prosperity, has the largest Communist party on this side of what used to be called the Iron Curtain. Many members of the Italian Communist Party are merely young people in revolt against interference by the Church in what would seem elsewhere to be the sphere of non-denominational politics. They resent being called upon to render unto God the things that are Caesar's.

Yet again, the centuries of civil war, of fierce campaigns by Italians in one city state against Italians in another, have left a distrust between regions, provinces and even small towns that goes far beyond the local jealousies one finds in other countries.

Lastly, one should realise the effect upon the Italian character of the great mass of mountains that cut Italy off from the rest of Europe. Ancient Rome and the Rome of early Christianity encouraged foreigners to cross the Alps when there were no railways and no proper roads; the Italians, except those whom unemployment drove abroad, had not the same incentive to tackle the difficult and dangerous mountain passes. The result has been that, although the Italians have been the victims of the foreign policies of other nations, they have been slow and uncertain in the development of a foreign policy of their own. They fought in both world wars, but they intervened so late or so unwisely that they received very few of the rewards they had expected after the first world war, and their disappointment led to a bitter reaction that enabled Mussolini to win their admiration, their adoration, by promising to trample democracy

underfoot. Democracy was so new; Fascism bore so many re-
semblances to the swaggering and swashbuckling past of the
condottieri, of the Visconti, the Montefeltro, the Gonzaga and
all the rest of them. It was obvious that Mussolini would be
more attracted by the bombastic boasts of Hitler than by the
gentle and reasoned arguments of the members of the League of
Nations Council, even though he must sometimes have recalled
the violent deaths of Julius Caesar and of so many other dic-
tators in the long history of his own country.

His end – with his body and that of his faithful mistress,
Clara Petacci, hung by the feet in a square in Milan – was typical
of so many violent deaths in Italy's turbulent history. His
legacy to his country has certainly not been to its advantage.
Many Italians learned of his death with thanksgiving, for they
had gone into exile or had taken to the hills as partisans rather
than serve him and his German masters. Many others learned
of it with fear, for they had continued as Fascists, some still
with enthusiasm and many more with resignation because it re-
quired courage to renounce a political doctrine that had helped
their careers and had given them power. Despite the haste
with which they assured everybody else that they had always
been anti-Fascist in their hearts, the period of Fascism has been
yet one more cause of distrust between one Italian and another,
not, thank God, to be compared with the old distrust between a
Guelf and a Ghibelline, but enough to bedevil the nation's
politics. Not enough, however, to interfere with the genuine
kindness shown by the Italians to the millions of foreigners who
so nearly crowd them off their own beaches.

2. Lucca and the Marble Mountains

A few miles south of La Spezia, on the west coast, the mountains that give so much beauty to the French and Italian Rivieras suddenly recede. In the course of centuries three rivers, the Magra, the Serchio and the Arno have brought down so much silt that they have formed a fertile plain, flanked by a beach that stretches for roughly 60 kilometres, to the mouth of the Arno. It is very wide, but in summer very crowded, for it includes well-known resorts such as Marina di Massa, Forte dei Marmi, Pietrasanta, Lido di Camaiore and Viareggio. It used to be famous for its background of stone pines, but within the last few years many of the trees have been killed by some pollution carried by the sea winds. To this, however, the holiday-makers, burnt brown or shocking pink, pay little attention. They lie in rows of deck-chairs provided by an endless line of bathing establishments (which add a lot to the holiday bill but do assure that the beach is clean and tidy) and they move only for a bathe or a drink outside some café. And in the evening they can go to what the Italians call a 'night' to listen to some 'big' in the entertainment world.

Some three to six kilometres behind this stretch of holiday beach, known as La Versilia, lies one of the least known but most dramatic regions in all Italy north of Rome. Every traveller by train, car, motorcycle or push-bike along this coast in daylight must have stared in astonishment at the mountains, apparently deep in snow even at the height of summer. The

Apennines, stretching all the way down the peninsula, with lateral ribs that end in rocky headlands between the long beaches, normally have bare but rounded summits, but these mountains behind Carrara have jagged peaks like those of the Alps and the Dolomites. The very name, Carrara, of course, explains why they appear to be covered with snow – the whiteness consists of millions of crystalline marble chips that have collected during the 2,000 years that have elapsed since man first began to quarry the marble. And their difference from the Apennines is emphasised by the fact that they are called Alps – Apuan Alps. They are not exceptionally high – a little under 2,000 metres at their highest – but they look very impressive since they rise from land that is little above sea-level.

Two paragraphs about marble, which one sees stacked on every otherwise vacant space between the mountains and the sea. Michelangelo spent months clambering around the quarries to select the right stone for his work. The huge block from which he carved his *David* came (after another Florentine sculptor, Bandinelli, had decided he could do nothing with it) originally from the Polvaccia quarry, four miles from Carrara, whereas the marble for his *Pietà* came from the mountains above Pietrasanta. (Pietrasanta means 'holy stone', and one wonders whether stone has ever been put to a holier purpose.) Over one-third of the world's marble comes from these Apuan Alps and, since the deposits are estimated to go down to a depth of 1,300 metres (4,225 feet), there is no immediate danger of a shortage of the raw material. The whitest marble is quarried at the greatest heights, and much of the best Carrara marble comes from a height of 1,749 metres (5,632 feet). Other minerals – for example, onyx from Pakistan – are brought to this region to be carved.

Down on the plain are numerous workshops, where visitors can see the marble being cut – sometimes in large sheets so thin that, unless they are stacked properly, they may warp. A visit to one of the studios may be difficult to organise and in any case the likelihood of seeing one of the world's great sculptors

6   *Pisa: the cathedral, from the Leaning Tower*

at work is small, although almost every one of them has had dealings with one or other of the Carrara studios. Unknown but very skilled workers make a clay copy of the sculptor's very small model and put nails into it at significant places and then, by measuring and multiplying the distance between these nails, reproduce the sculptor's inspiration at the desired size. Many a sculptor never sees his full-size statue, which will be unveiled with pomp, ceremony and praise in some distant country, until he comes to Carrara or Pietrasanta to carve his name on its pedestal. Watching the men at work in one of the studios, one realises how great the competition must have been to become an apprentice in the studio of an artist such as Michelangelo and how much may have been accomplished by other chisels than his own. Now the work is made much easier by power-driven drills and chisels, but one is filled with respect for the craftsmen who use them.

Behind these Apuan Alps, and between them and the Apennines, is a region of singular beauty, generally known as the Garfagnana, although the strict regionalist would claim that only a part of the region deserves that name. This is the valley of two rivers – the Aulella, which flows northwards to the Magra, and the Serchio which reaches the sea 12 kilometres north of the Arno. None of the guide books I have consulted even mentions the Garfagnana; they soon will.

One of the most beautiful drives I know anywhere in the world starts from Castelnuovo di Garfagnana, half-way along the road from Fivizzano at the northern end of this valley of two rivers, and Bagni di Lucca, near its southern end. The mountain road I recommend goes from Castelnuovo (where the poet Ariosto was governor from 1522 to 1525) to the sea at Pietrasanta. It passes under the northern side of Monte Pania (1,858 metres), past a deeply-green little lake, and through a long dark tunnel to a stupendous view of the Versilia plain and the Tyrrhenian sea. Interest is added to beauty by the marble quarries where workmen are cutting huge blocks out of the cliff. These blocks are now transported to the workshops on

7 *Elba: Portoferraio, from the castle*

lorries: in Michelangelo's day most of them either slid down the slopes to the valley or were let down on sledges, held back by ropes wound round stanchions. The life of a quarryman was dangerous, whatever the method used.

In the early days of Christianity, when thousands of pilgrims made the perilous journey to Rome, they followed the valleys of the Aulella and the Serchio to Lucca, and one of the churches I would advise you to visit, high up in the Garfagnana mountains, contains the bones of San Pellegrino, an Irish saint who devoted his life to guiding pilgrims on their way. One road to San Pellegrino is now an excellent road that links Modena to Lucca; another road, which I followed with a friend in search of summer pastures for his sheep, consisted of large, flat stones – the old Roman road. Caesar's legionaries may have marched here long before the advent of the pilgrims. The Romans had great difficulty in conquering the Ligurians who lived in this wild region of the Apuan Alps. Some they eventually drove north of the Magra river, which became the northern frontier of Italy; others they took all the way down to the mountains of the Abruzzi, where they settled. The Garfagnana is still wild country, which gave concealment to many British escaped prisoners of war. I am not surprised that, in the fifteenth and sixteenth centuries, the Garfagnana's annual tribute to the state of Modena was a bear.

People in the Garfagnana know very much more about the British and the Americans than the British and the Americans know about them. As in many other parts of Italy, one comes across 'Americani' and is surprised to discover that, though they do indeed have American passports, their knowledge of the language is rudimentary. They are generally elderly men – men who migrated to the States when they were young, and worked there until they had earned their American old age pensions, which allow them to return to the village where they were born and to live there in relative luxury. But the Garfagnana has other migrants who have come home. For generations the region was famous for a cottage industry producing little plaster figurines, much more religious, more elegant, but less colourful than the Staffordshire figures one used to see on mantelpieces in English cottages and now sees in the shop windows of antique dealers. With trays of these attractive little figures balanced on their heads, the young men of the Garfagnana went from town to town in country after country. Some of them settled abroad, and others married foreign girls and brought them back to their native mountains.

For some reason, these itinerant vendors did best in Glasgow. Figurines are no longer fashionable there, but ice creams and fish and chips are popular. Many of the Glaswegians who sell them came originally from Garfagnana. Many have married Scots, and it is not at all unusual, in some small mountain village of the Garfagnana, to hear two women gossiping in broad Scottish accents.

The chief town in the region is Barga, which can trace its records back to the year 754. Its history is filled with accounts of its many subsequent revolts against authority, involving sieges by the armies of Lucca, of Florence, of Pisa and other city states. It is now a charming and quiet summer resort. Almost unknown is the church of San Francesco, just below the town, which has some remarkable Della Robbias – probably by Andrea though the people of Barga attribute them to the more famous Luca, Andrea's uncle. The Della Robbias had a furnace in which they baked their *terrecotte* in the valley below Barga. Their success is believed to have provided the inspiration for the development of the plaster figurines.

The little town has two considerable attractions for the tourist – an incomparable view of the rugged Apuan Alps, just across the valley, and a splendid cathedral which contains a very remarkable pulpit. It is large and square, and it rests on four orange-coloured marble columns. The front two columns in turn rest on the backs of two lions, one of which is trampling on a winged dragon and the other is attacking a man who tries to defend himself by stabbing the lion with his sword. (One finds this motif in many churches in this area; I write a little

more about them in the section dealing with Lucca.) A third
attraction of Barga each August is provided by a remarkable
school of opera, founded some years ago by two British residents, Peter and Gillian Hunt. At the end of their course, the
students from several countries give performances of operas
in Barga's charming eighteenth-century *Teatro dei Differ-
enti.*

Two more paragraphs about the Garfagnana. If you are driving southwards from Barga and towards Lucca, go half a mile
off the main road to visit Ghivizzano. You must leave your
car outside its one and only gate, for the streets are very narrow,
but it is one of the best examples of a *'castello'*, as they called
the small, walled towns of the Middle Ages, and it was also the
birthplace of Castruccio Castracani degli Antelminelli, Duke of
Lucca and Pistoia and one of the greatest of the condottieri, the
leaders of the mercenary armies that did so much of the
fighting in Italy in the days of wars between the rival princi-
palities. He was not, perhaps, as famous as Gattamelata of Padua,
Colleoni of Bergamo, Sigismondo Malatesta of Rimini, or the
Englishman, Sir John Hawkwood of Florence, but he was a great
leader of men, and less mercenary than most. He died in 1328
at the age of 47, just when it seemed probable that he could become ruler of the whole of Tuscany. As for Ghivizzano, 'the
streets are the streets he made, and as curious as any in Christen-
dom. One of them runs round inside the walls and is roofed over
all the way, and only lighted by narrow loopholes made for
shooting from.' (*Lucca: Mediaeval Towns Series*, Dent, London.)

The tourist on his way down to Lucca should also visit Bagni
di Lucca in the deep valley of the River Lima. The waters of the
three villages that form this little spa have been well known for
centuries. The Emperor Frederick II – '*Stupor Mundi*' – visited it
in 1245 – although there was no reasonable road to it until one
was built on the orders of Napoleon's sister, Elisa Baciocchi,
whom he had appointed to rule Lucca in 1805. In the last century it was one of the most fashionable resorts, and it attracted
Montaigne, Heine, Lamartine, James Stuart (son of James II), the

8   *San Gimignano: the towers*

Brownings, Tennyson and, of course, those indefatigable travellers, Byron and Shelley. A once famous but now forgotten writer who survived into the present century and whose long sojourn at Bagni di Lucca is recalled by a plaque outside her house, was 'Ouida', whose romantic novels caused thousands of Edwardian hearts to flutter. Undoubtedly the waters of Bagni di Lucca are just as health-giving today as ever they were, but fashion has passed by this charming and elegant little town. The tourist should not pass it by, however, even though the English church, once so crowded on Sunday mornings by 'somebodies' now stands empty and forgotten.

Lucca, on the *autostrada* from Florence to the west coast, is one of half a dozen places north of Rome which, in my opinion, are absurdly neglected by foreigners who wish to know Italy without discomfort. The city has no ruined castle, commemorating some robber baron whose family acquired wealth and culture at the expense of the people over whom it ruled; its past is symbolised rather by the watch towers on the surrounding hills, on which fires were lit to warn citizens of approaching enemies. It was of necessity involved in many wars with Pisa, Florence, Pistoia, Siena and other city states but, from the fourteenth century onwards, the periods when the citizens had no say in their government were very short. It was a proud little republic, contributing its own independent force to the first Crusade, minting its own money (which, with that of Pavia, was for a time the most widely accepted currency in the whole country) and weaving silks that were in great demand all over Europe. The result is that the hills around the city have a variety of elegant patrician villas that is possibly unrivalled in any other region except around Florence itself and along the Brenta Canal, where the wealthy Venetian merchants used to have their country houses. It has, I suppose, a longer history as an independent republic than anywhere else in Italy except the Republic of San Marino, which has retained a remarkable degree of independence since the year 885.

9   *Siena: the cathedral across the ancient part of the city*

Lucca comes into recorded history in 218 B.C. when Consul Sempronius took refuge there after his defeat by Hannibal. It acquired fame in 56 B.C. when Julius Caesar, Pompey and Crassus, the three most important Romans of their time, met there and decided how they were going to run Rome and its possessions. The most central church, San Michele in Foro, gets its name from the fact that the square in which it stands used to be the Roman forum. One can imagine these three men pacing up and down there while they discussed their plans. The place is now the meeting place of farmers who come there twice a week, as their ancestors must have done for nearly 2,000 years, and of tourists who stare up at San Michele's extraordinary Pisan-Romanesque façade. This façade, which is much higher than the roof of the basilica itself – money must have run short – is bewildering in its variety of carving, basically twelfth-century, but much of it restored and some of it modern – high up among the rows of heads is the portrait of one of the creators of united Italy, Garibaldi; his presence there is at least surprising when one remembers his campaign against the pope for national unity. But the façade merits a study through field-glasses when the afternoon sun lights up its details. Even without glasses or sunshine it has its fascinations – just over the main doorway, for example, there are delightful dragons and a centaur, the human half of which grows out of the middle of its back.

An even more attractive façade is that of the cathedral of San Martino, constructed by Guidetto da Como in 1210. (Note the fact that it is jammed so closely to the great tower that the right-hand arch is smaller and narrower than the other two.) The façade is less imposing than those of the cathedral in Pisa and of San Michele in Lucca, but the variety of its carvings is even more fascinating. The members of the Comacine Guild, stone-masons from the Lake of Como, decorated everything they made with comical human figures, legendary animals, interlaced foliage and geometrical patterns. Note the small man crouching beneath the weight of the arch near the tower (very similar to the little man supporting one of the rear columns of the pulpit in Barga); the angel blowing his trumpet under the corbel, also in the right-hand corner; the two men, under the corbel holding up the front legs of St Martin's horse, who appear to be swallowing dragons by their tails.

The decoration of these Romanesque churches by the Comacine Guild often seems grotesque and childish – what have all these animals, many killing each other, to do with a Christian church? Apparently they are all symbolic. The two men, for example, are not swallowing dragons by their tails; they are gossips and slanderers, and the dragons represent the evil words issuing from their mouths. But there are great differences of opinion about the meaning of many of these symbols. To some, the hunted stag denotes pride on the point of receiving the punishment it deserves; to others, it denotes the soul fleeing from temptation. The bear, the dragon and the wolf represent evil while the wild boar represents greed, but the lion is much more puzzling. As the king of beasts, it is often held to represent the Lion of Judah, but the Comacine Guild frequently portrayed it in the act of killing a human being (generally a knight in armour) who is simultaneously stabbing a knife into its stomach. That, surely, is not the way for the Lion of Judah to behave? The members of this guild carved lions by the hundred – the nicest one I have seen anywhere, looking exactly like a carica-ture of an infuriated major, is above a shop at the corner of Lucca's main shopping street, the Fillungo, and a narrow passage called the Chiasso Barletti. For about two centuries from the beginning of the eleventh century, the lion was generally on top of a column; thereafter it was crouching down to support one.

I hesitate to be dogmatic about works of art, but I doubt whether anything else in the Duomo is as beautiful as the tomb of Ilaria del Caretto, one of the earliest but certainly one of the finest works by Jacopo della Quercia, the greatest of Siena's sculptors. I know of no other work of sculpture which gives one such a deep feeling of repose and peace, even though I cannot quite share Ruskin's opinion that anyone who studied it for a long time 'would, I believe, receive such a lesson of love as no coldness could refuse, no fatuity forget and no insolence disobey'. Ilaria was the wife of Paolo Guinigi whose town house, built in the fourteenth century, is conspicuous on account of the trees that grow on the top of its tower, and whose family became so unpopular as the dominating family in a state the motto of which is '*Libertas*' that parts of this beautiful tomb were sold and the rest was relegated to a humble position in a very remote chapel. The missing parts were recovered and the tomb placed in its present site in the north transept only in 1840. Paolo Guinigi himself was imprisoned by the Milanese ruler, Visconti, in Pavia, where he died at the age of 59.

But the principal treasure of the cathedral is, of course, the '*Volto Santo*' or 'Holy Countenance', a wooden figure of Christ on the cross, in a little octagonal chapel built by Matteo Civitali, Lucca's most famous sculptor. The legends attached to the *Volto Santo* at one time made it so famous that several kings of France and William II of England took their oath '*par le Saint Voult de Lucques*' and pilgrims came to Lucca in their thousands to pray before it.

The legend of its origin deserves repetition. It was carved out of cedar wood by Nicodemus, who helped to bury Jesus after the Crucifixion, and it remained hidden in a cave for several centuries. An Italian bishop had a vision in which he learned of its whereabouts and he put it on a ship without a crew. Despite this handicap, the ship sailed away and finally appeared off the coast near Luni, the Roman fortress near Bocca di Magra. For days, crews in Genoese ships tried in vain to capture this crewless vessel. Giovanni, the Bishop of Lucca, was ordered in a vision to go down to the beach. The Bishop of Luni was already there and had promised absolution to any man who could get the ship under control. When told of Giovanni's vision, he asked for one more day during which his men would continue their efforts. 'All day and all night the Genoese and the people of Luni tried to take her but, without going far from the port of Luni she ever escaped them, hither and thither, now here, now there.'

Lucca's turn had come. The bishop called upon his people to kneel on the sand, then 'he stretched out his arms with great devotion towards the ship, and with his hand drew her to earth as though she had been a feather'. Besides the *Volto Santo*, the ship contained one of the nails of the Cross, a phial containing Jesus's blood and the sheet in which his Body had been wrapped when laid in the tomb. Giovanni presented the phial to the Bishop of Luni, and prepared to take the *Volto Santo*. But the local people were dissatisfied, so he suggested that the statue should be placed on a cart drawn by two unbroken steers, which would go where God willed them to go. This was agreed, and the steers immediately headed for Lucca, possibly encouraged to do so by the fact that the bishop and his clergy walked ahead of them. The steers stopped of their own accord outside San Martino, and the statue was erected in a special chapel built in the middle of the piazza. This was in the year 742. Later, it was placed inside the Cathedral where it attracted so many pilgrims from all over Europe that a special tribunal was instituted to hear the complaints of pilgrims that they had been cheated by the money-changers who had stalls under the portico.

One Lucca church has especial interest for the Irish and the English. This is the church built in the twelfth century in honour of the city's greatest saint, San Frediano, who was Bishop of Lucca from 560 to 578, and who is believed also to be St Finnian of Moville, in Ireland. He is buried under the high altar. He was responsible for the building of several lovely churches in the neighbourhood, but he is remembered less for these good works than for the legend that, when the people appealed to him for help to prevent the annual flooding of Lucca by the River Serchio, he took an ordinary garden rake, and ordered the river to follow him away from the city walls. Which it did. This achievement is recorded in a rather poor painting by Amico Aspertini in the second chapel on the left (where is also a painting to illustrate the *Volto Santo* on its way from Luni to Lucca). San Frediano's miracle with the garden rake is also commemorated in one of the north windows of the Cathedral.

Under the altar – another work by Jacopo della Quercia – in the fourth chapel on the left is a sarcophagus which is alleged to contain the bones of 'Saint Richard, King of England'. And if you do not know much about this saintly king, nor does anybody else. Some experts say that he was a son of King Offa of Mercia, others that his father was King of Wessex, and that he was born in Devonshire; yet others that he was the son of a Hampshire farmer. His epitaph, which John Evelyn copied down in 1645, has disappeared; it stated that '*rex fuit Anglorum*' but that he had abdicated in order to devote his life to Christ. He was the father of St Willibald, St Winebald and St Walburga. He died in Lucca in 722, during a pilgrimage to Rome. Four saints in two generations must be nearly a record.

A third saint is buried in San Frediano – Santa Zita, the patron saint of servant girls, who, in the thirteenth century, was a little free with the belongings of her employer, a wealthy silk merchant, for the benefit of the poor. For example, one day she was smuggling out of the house a basket full of eggs. Her mistress snatched away a napkin that covered them, and the eggs had miraculously turned into flowers. On her saint's day, 27 April, the square in front of San Frediano becomes a beautiful show of flowers and plants in a beautiful setting. As the Guide Michelin would put it, this event '*Vaut le détour*'. On this occasion, Santa Zita's skeleton in its glass case is on display in the nave of the church, and the faithful, or the superstitious, buy flowers with which they stroke the glass. Personally, I find more interesting the large twelfth-century font just outside her chapel. Among the carvings on its upper part is one head which might be the work of Picasso since it shows a man both full-face and side-face at the same time. The lower half has a fascinating set of figures all round it. Among them is an army of Israelites or Egyptians, clad in mediaeval armour, crossing the Red Sea.

(There is a very similar carving in Salona, Yugoslavia, showing the Israelites safely across but the Egyptians in grave difficulties.) Note that in San Frediano one horse has to carry two knights, and that the knight at the back has his knees turned in the direction of the horse's tail, whereas his shoulders and head are turned towards the horse's head.

At the far end of the little piazza in front of San Frediano is the Fillungo, which has the advantage over most streets that wheeled traffic is banned from much of its length. Before you turn into it, look back at San Frediano, with its severely beautiful façade surmounted by an ancient mosaic (restored in 1829), its splendid, wide steps and its tower, typical in this part of Italy in that the number of its windows increases with its height. This, to my mind, is one of the most satisfying views in Lucca.

On the far side of the Fillungo (which, in consonance with its name, stretches like a long thread almost from one gate of the town to the other) is the Roman amphitheatre, several columns of which are now in San Frediano. This has come down in the world – instead of being an empty but tidy ruin as are most Roman amphitheatres today, it is a busy fruit and vegetable market and its loggias are little better than slum dwellings. Only the oval shape of the arena and the great blocks of Roman masonry still showing in the outside wall reveal the building's original purpose. It thus escapes the attention of many tourists, and some people are in favour of turning it back into the ruin it must have been in the seventh century, or whenever it was that enthusiastic church builders pulled it to pieces. To me, on the contrary, it is far more impressive as it is today, when its patchwork of Roman and modern brick, its windows and its built-in arches, give one a sense of continuity. The people crowding through the entrances to see some imposing spectacle eighteen centuries ago were the ancestors of the salesmen laying out their fruit and vegetables on their market stalls or living in rooms one wall of which was built during the great days of the Roman Empire. If you notice the proportions of the arch over

one of the main entrances to the amphitheatre, it will be
obvious to you that, during the intervening centuries, the level
of the ground has been raised by eight feet or so – in some parts
of ancient Rome, the original pavement is said to lie some 40
feet below the present surface, for each generation tends to
build on some of its own rubbish.

Only a few huge stones are left to show where were the
city's original Roman walls. Lucca outgrew them, and new
walls, of which two fine gateways remain, were built in the
thirteenth century. But, enclosing a still larger city, are the
walls that make Lucca unique. They date from the sixteenth
and seventeenth centuries, and are so complete that a motor
road, lined by great chestnuts and plane trees, goes all the way
round the top of them. Inside this kind of Maginot line there
are corridors, store rooms and halls of which some are so large
that concerts or exhibitions are housed in them during the
summer. From these walls there are magnificent views of the
old city – in particular of San Frediano and the Cathedral – and
from almost every narrow street inside the city, you have a
refreshing view of the trees that grow on them. I believe that
the walls were never needed in the defence of Lucca except
on one occasion when the gates were shut to lessen the impact
of flood water – San Frediano's little rake has not been so effective as one likes to pretend.

3. Pisa to Florence

Lucca attracts too few tourists; Pisa, 19 kilometres away to the south-west, attracts too many. I should guess that the cars parked within 200 metres of the Leaning Tower display a greater variety of foreign number plates than could be found in any other comparable area in the world. Its two original architects, Bonanno Pisano and William of Innsbruck, began to build it in 1173, but work seems to have been abandoned because the foundations were sinking on one side. Two other architects took up the task in 1275, and the tower was finished in 1350.

The tower is not very high – 55 metres, compared with 132 metres to the top of the cross on St Peter's, Rome – but that fact makes the inclination of more than four metres out of the perpendicular all the more remarkable. Pisa is only a few feet above sea-level, and the subsoil consists mainly of sand. The tower weighs some 15,000 tons. One can therefore understand the care with which every new millimetre of inclination is checked and the efforts that are constantly being made to strengthen its foundations. The experience of climbing almost 300 steps to the top is not to be recommended to everyone; each time I have climbed them I have felt a little seasick, since the floor of each storey is more than 60 centimetres lower on one side than on the other. I climb them nevertheless since I am fascinated by the details of the neighbouring cathedral when seen from above.

Galileo Galilei, the famous astronomer and philosopher, was

born in Pisa, and the guides like to tell you that he made his discovery about the velocity of falling bodies by dropping things from the Leaning Tower. This, however, the experts now deny, as they also deny that the lamp which hangs near the pulpit in the cathedral existed when he discovered that the range of the swing, or oscillation, has no effect on its duration. (It is, however, quite possible that he made this discovery, which gave us the pendulum clock, by watching a lamp which previously hung there.)

The cathedral, built partly with the help of six shiploads of loot brought back from a successful attack on Palermo in 1063, is in the style known as Pisan Romanesque. It is in white marble, with alternating horizontal strips of coloured marble and with small arcades, one above the other – a style in great favour in this part of Italy in the eleventh and twelfth centuries. The bronze door of the south transept – the door through which worshippers are normally admitted – is the work of Bonanno Pisano, and its twenty-four panels admirably represent scenes from the Scriptures. Giovanni Pisano's pulpit is world-famous. It is generally considered the best of the four pulpits associated with the Pisano family, the first of which is in the Baptistery, and which was the work of his father, Niccolà.

For me, the greatest attraction of Pisa is the Campo Santo, just near the cathedral and the imposing, octagonal Baptistery. For some weeks during the war, the Allies were on the south bank of the Arno and the Germans on the north. Most of the fine buildings facing the river were therefore destroyed – one recaptures the former beauty of this wide sweep of the river only on the evening of 16 June, when the bridges and buildings are lit up by thousands upon thousands of candles in glasses, in honour of St Ranieri, Pisa's patron saint. Although the Cathedral, the Baptistery and the Leaning Tower stand isolated from all other buildings by wide lawns, and might therefore have been badly damaged by shell-fire, they escaped almost undamaged.

But the Campo Santo was less fortunate. A shell set fire to the beams of the roof, and the heat melted the sheets of lead that rested on them. The molten lead irrevocably damaged some of the most attractive frescoes in all Italy, and notably Benozzo Gozzoli's scenes from the Old Testament and Traini's 'Triumph of Death'. Enough, however, remains and has been restored with great patience and skill to make a visit to the Campo Santo a 'must'. At any rate, a 'must' for me. Inside this Campo Santo there hangs an immense chain which at one time protected the port of Pisa against invaders. It was taken away by the Genoese in 1284, after the defeat of the Pisans in the Battle of Meloria, a small island off Leghorn, which put an end to Pisa as a rival to Genoa and Venice for the mastery of the Mediterranean. The Genoese also took so many prisoners that there was a saying: '*Chi vuol' veder Pisa, vada a Genova*' – 'He who wants to see Pisa must go to Genoa'. After Italy became united in 1860, Genoa restored the chain, but so much silt has come down the River Arno in later centuries that the city is now some miles from the sea. There is now no port to be defended.

The Piazza dei Cavalieri, half-way between the Arno and the Cathedral, is surely one of the most beautiful squares in Tuscany. The buildings round it date back to different centuries, but each of them is attractive in its way. The church, Santo Stefano dei Cavalieri, is, by Italian standards, almost modern, since it was built at the end of the sixteenth century for the knights of a new Order of Chivalry, the Order of St Stephen, established by the Grand Duke Cosimo de' Medici (whose equestrian statue stands in front of the neighbouring Palazzo Conventuale dei Cavalieri, now a famous college). The knights were created partly to provide Cosimo with a new aristocracy, most members of the old one having been exiled or eliminated, and partly to check the piracy that was playing such merry hell with Florence's overseas trade.

On the north side of the square, there is still part of the building in the tower of which, in 1288, the Ghibellines imprisoned the Guelf Count Ugolino della Gherardesca, his sons and his nephew, and starved them to death. For days, passersby could hear them crying out for food and for absolution. The archbishop's reaction to their appeals was to have the key to their tower thrown into the Arno. It is, nevertheless, a beautiful square.

Many motorists who travel from Pisa to Florence now avoid the main road, via Pontedera and Empoli, because it has to carry so much heavy traffic. Instead, they take the *autostrada* from the coast to Florence. Thereby they miss the opportunity of turning off the main road to the right, to San Miniato, or to the left, to Vinci. San Miniato is a charming little hill-town capped by one enormous red-brick tower, which is all that remains of a great castle, built quite possibly more than a thousand years ago, to enable the Holy Roman Emperors to control one of the most important road junctions in Central Italy – the point where the road from Florence to Pisa and the sea crossed the so-called Via Francigena, which left the Via Emilia at Parma, crossed the mountains over the Cisa Pass, went down the Serchio valley to Lucca, crossed the Arno between San Miniato and Fucecchio, and followed the Via Cassia along the Val d'Elsa to Siena and the south.

San Miniato became so important to the Holy Roman Emperors that they stationed a strong garrison of German troops there, which explains why the place is still known as San Miniato al Tedesco. Both the great Hohenstaufen rulers, Frederick Barbarossa and his grandson, Frederick II ('*Stupor Mundi*') stayed at San Miniato.

The tower is, in fact, brand new – it is an exact copy of the old tower, which was destroyed during the last war. But the visitor who has climbed up to the foot of it has little reason to complain; from the hill-top of San Miniato he has a stupendous view, with the plain of the Arno (rendered hideous by haphazard building) at his feet on the north side and, to south, east and west, as lovely a panorama of hills and valleys and old, red-brown roofs as any Renaissance artist painted as a background for one of his pictures. On a very clear day, according to that great lover of Tuscany, the late Edward Hutton, you can see 'distant Montecatini and Pistoia under the towering waves of the Apennines, Monte Cimone leaping sky high and the range surging away to Monte Morello above Florence'. Some of this I find difficult to believe – how can one see Pistoia, with the great bulk of Monte Albano in the way? – but I can believe that, to the west, you can see 'Lucca and Pisa with a shimmer of distant sea' and, to the south-west and south, Volterra and San Gimignano. In any case, a superb view.

The turning off the main road to the left, to Vinci, is rather less rewarding. The museum, in an impressive old castle, shuts from twelve to four, and it is probably between these hours that most people, on their way to and from more important towns, would be likely to make the détour. A mile or so farther up the hill-side, at Anchiano, is an attractive old house, of which a part belonged to the Vinci family : (the rest is of more recent date). It is here that Leonardo probably was born and certainly spent some of his boyhood. His father was a very well-known Florentine notary, four times married, but not to Leonardo's mother, a woman in humble circumstances. But this accident of illegitimacy did not prevent the boy from being brought up with Ser Piero's many other children. The house is on the hill-side in a country of olives; since olive trees live for many centuries, I suppose some of them on that hill-side may have been there when Leonardo was a boy.

Travellers who reject this old road from Pisa to Florence, and prefer to take the *autostrada* too readily resist any temptation to go off it to visit Lucca – unless I happen to have aroused their curiosity in the previous chapter – Montecatini, Pistoia or Prato. They are in too much of a hurry to get to their Florentine hotel, and it must be admitted that the authorities do little to encourage them to delay, for much of the land on either side of the *autostrada* is classed as a 'depressed area' and tax concessions are given to manufacturers who will build their factories upon it.

Montecatini has all the assets of a famous health resort – good doctors, good hotels, and so on – but also all the disadvantages, chief of which is that too many people there want to discuss their ailments. But the mountains to the north of it, rising to 1,388 metres at the winter sports resort of Abetone, are covered with chestnut and beech forests, and even have a herd of moufflon, the wild sheep now normally found only in Sardinia; a few were brought from that island some years ago, and now number at least 100. It was across this wild country that ran the Gothic Line, the last great system of German defences in the last war, and these woods provided hiding places for scores of escaped prisoners of war.

Pistoia (where pistols are said to have been invented; hence their name) is well worth a visit. Its Piazza del Duomo, with the Cathedral, the Baptistery, the Palazzo del Comune and the Palazzo Pretorio, is very impressive, and serves to remind one that this peaceful little town has a very important past. The Pistoiese forces were involved in many wars with those of Florence, Pisa and Lucca, and a most improbable legend claims that in 1305, when they were being besieged by the armies of both Florence and Lucca, the Pistoiese tried to prolong their defence by cutting off their own limbs and eating them. The armorial bearings on the walls of its public buildings indicate its former wealth. A feud between two Pistoiese families split the Guelf party into Blacks and Whites, one consequence of which was that Dante, a Guelf but a supporter of the Whites, was exiled by the Blacks from Florence.

Pistoia has several beautiful churches besides the Duomo and the Baptistery. Sant' Andrea and San Giovanni Fuorcivitas are both remarkable examples of Pisan style of Lombard architecture, resembling the Duomo and San Michele in Lucca and, oddly enough, at least one church in Bari, in the deep South. The Duomo contains a remarkable silver altar, to which several different silversmiths contributed from 1287 over a period of nearly two centuries. One ought not to leave Pistoia without seeing the work of another family of famous artists, the glazed terracotta frieze on the façade of the Hospital del Ceppo. This is partly the work of Giovanni della Robbia – in some ways even more effective than the much more famous Andrea della Robbia medallions outside the Foundling Hospital in Florence. (Luca della Robbia invented this method of glazing sculptured terracotta in the fifteenth century. Andrea was his nephew, and Giovanni and Girolamo were his sons.)

Prato, where the north–south *Autostrada del Sole* crosses the one which links Florence with the Tyrrhenian Sea, was to the artists of the Early Renaissance what Barbizon was to the French painters towards the end of last century. Almost all the great artists of the period came there, and many of them left some of their work behind them. The open-air pulpit at a corner of the Cathedral is the joint work of Donatello and Michelozzi. It was in Prato that Fra Filippo Lippi, from the Carmelite monastery in Florence, painted a very beautiful novice as his model for the Madonna. One result was that he painted one of the most beautiful Madonnas ever produced. Another result was that he and his model produced an illegitimate baby. They were, however, later permitted to marry and the child became Filippino Lippi, an artist nearly as famous as his father.

For centuries, Prato has been an important centre for the textile industry, and, as you drive past it along the *autostrada*, you may see huge bundles of rags. You may also see these huge bundles lying among the olive groves up in the hills, for the rags are valuable when dug in round the tree to retain whatever moisture there is during the long, dry summers.

Near the junction of the two *autostrade* there is a church with a sagging roof – designedly so : it is supposed to represent a tent, and it was built in memory of workmen who lost their lives while the *autostrade* were being built. Before going on your way to Florence, it might be worth your while to visit it; it is an example of very modern architecture. Most of my friends dislike it intensely : I like it very much.

By now, Prato is almost a suburb of Florence, and one approaches the City of the Lily in a mood of growing apprehen-

sion. But suddenly, beyond and above the ugly disorder of factories and blocks of flats, one sees Brunelleschi's great dome and
Giotto's great tower. One sees Florence.

> *Here is Botticelli's dream that shone*
> *With del Sarto's skill, Angelico's pure fire,*
> *Da Vinci's science, Savonarola's creed.*

(Richard Church, *North of Rome*, Hutchinson, London, 1960)

10   *Orvieto: a distant view of the town*

4. The Via Aurelia

The most obvious way from Pisa to Rome is, of course, along the coast, which is the way the Roman soldiers marched on their return from some campaign in Spain or southern France. It is not, however, the way I would recommend, for much of it is flat, dull and lacking in architectural or historical interest. For centuries, it was avoided like the plague since travellers there were, in fact, likely to contract a disease that caused many deaths. In the nineteenth century, everybody making the Grand Tour was very careful to reach Rome before dark, and a certain Miss Starke wrote of the *campagna* round Rome that it was 'ill-cultivated and worse drained, so that fogs and igneous vapours prevail during the night; it likewise abounds with sulphur, arsenic and vitriol'. What *did* prevail in the Campagna and in the Maremma farther north was malaria, caused not, as the name suggests, by bad air, but by the anopheles mosquito, so that the flat lands along the west coast, now of immense agricultural value, were nearly deserted. They are therefore much less interesting for the visitor than the hill towns of the interior, about which I have written in other chapters – San Miniato, San Gimignano, Siena, Volterra, Orvieto and Viterbo.

But the Via Aurelia, of course, provides the quickest road to Rome, and it is the one followed in this chapter.

Livorno (Leghorn), 13 miles south of Pisa, is not nearly as picturesque as a large port and ship-building centre ought to be. For one thing, it was very heavily bombed during the last

11 *Florence: a view from the roof of the Pitti palace*

war; for another, it is very much newer than most Italian cities; for yet another, it is a very busy industrial city, which is not the kind of city to which one comes for a holiday. It is, says Baedeker, 'uncompromisingly modern and has no important monuments of art' apart, perhaps, from the impressive monument of the *Quattro Mori*, a monument dating from 1624 to celebrate a victory over the Moors won by the Knights of St Stephen. Even the *Guida Rapida* of the Italian Touring Club writes that 'it calls for a visit of only a few hours'. The water front is pleasant enough, and I imagine that it is a pleasant town to live in, with its mountainous background and its many bathing establishments, and with the cadets of its Naval Academy to brighten its social life. But the tourist bound southwards from Pisa would be wise to take the inland road, via Collesalvetti, through pleasant, downland country, rejoining the Via Aurelia at Cecina, even though he will thereby miss more than 20 kilometres of rugged coastline immediately south of Leghorn, with two pretty and popular bathing resorts, Quercianella and Castiglioncello.

Historically Leghorn is interesting enough just because its history has been so short. Having been devastated at different times by the Saracens, the French, the Genoese, the Florentines and the Lucchesi, its population in 1551 was reduced to 749. It is now well over 150,000. How and why? I have already mentioned the way in which the Arno has brought down so much silt that Pisa is now some eleven kilometres from the open sea. By the seventeenth century, Porto Pisano (south of the present mouth of the river) had become almost useless, and Cosimo de' Medici decided that Tuscany needed a new and better port; he chose the impoverished village of Leghorn. He proclaimed it a free port and encouraged residents by making it a refuge, with no questions asked, for exiles from every country. Those who settled there included many Jews (mostly from Portugal or Spain), Greeks, Germans, Englishmen, Scots, Turks, Arabs and others. The British community was at one time so large that there was an English 'factory' – a social and business headquarters, such as the English established in many foreign ports – and the Protestant cemetery has many British tombs, one of them being that of Tobias Smollett, who died in Leghorn in 1771.

A tablet on part of the old fortifications that survived the bombing of the last war is a tribute to a strange Englishman who was made Earl of Warwick and Duke of Northumberland by the Holy Roman Emperor because he had served Tuscany so well and because he had little hope of getting his claim to these titles recognised by the King of England. He was Robert Dudley, son of Queen Elizabeth's favourite of the same name (whom she created Earl of Leicester) and grandson of the Duke of Northumberland. His morals were questionable, but he had a lot to do with the creation of the port of Leghorn and the draining of the Pisan marshes, as well as building ships and being useful to the Grand Duke of Tuscany in many other ways.

The coast road from Leghorn to Castiglioncello is beautiful. One's ambition thereafter is to get as quickly as possible to the next promontory, at the end of which is Piombino. Having reached Piombino, one wants to get away from it even more quickly, for it has immense steel works, with chimneys which belch out red and yellow smoke all day long. But I, for one, always see Piombino with pleasure, for it is the port from which the car ferry takes me across to Elba. People who are bound for Rome in a hurry miss Piombino and Elba altogether, for the Aurelia goes inland from San Vincenzo, a pleasant seaside resort but with no particular character, to Follonica, which merits a similar description with the addition that it also has smelting works. Thereafter, the road turns still farther inland to Grosseto, capital of the province, and finally back to the sea near Orbetello.

I revert to my beloved Elba, some ten kilometres from the mainland – *il continente*, as the Elbans always call it – and reached in a little over an hour by car ferries. The island is about 24 kilometres from east to west, and an average of nine kilometres from north to south, but its coastline has so many capes and bays, hills and valleys, that nobody seems to agree on its length, beyond saying that anyone walking round it would cover well over 100 kilometres. More than half the island is more than 150 metres above sea level, and on the same day I have found prickly pears near the sea and autumn cyclamens on the mountainside near the hermitage of the Madonna del Monte. It is said to be composed of more than 150 different minerals, so that many visitors return to the mainland weighed down by stones of one colour or another, each of which is twice as heavy as one would expect. Iron ore has been mined at the eastern end of the island since the days of the Etruscans, and the most popular mineral (found only by those who have permission to visit the mines) is 'fool's gold' – iron pyrites to the expert, but to the layman, gold in every respect except its value. The Etruscans had to take the ore to the source of fuel, namely the forests, and, although they sent most of the ore back to Populonia, on the mainland, if you scramble about on the hillsides you may come across a place where there are lumps of half-smelted ore from one of their furnaces.

Elba, of course, is best known for the fact that Napoleon was exiled there in May 1814, as a result of the disasters that befell him after his retreat from Moscow. He had been compelled to abdicate a few weeks before his arrival on Elba, but he had been permitted to retain his rank as monarch, although his kingdom had been reduced to this one small island. For some hours after his arrival at Portoferraio, the island's chief port, he remained on the British ship that had brought him there while one of his generals went ashore to find out whether the people were going to receive him with cheers or hisses. In fact, they were flattered to receive so famous a man; they hurriedly cleared the top floor of the Town Hall, borrowed furniture for it from the richer citizens, and met him on the quayside with the keys of the town.

Napoleon lived on the island for nine months, after which he escaped, arrived back in Paris, and became emperor again for

100 days. Then came Waterloo, and the final and much harsher exile on the island of St Helena. Within 24 hours of his arrival on Elba, he had dictated over 2,000 words concerning the government of his minute kingdom on matters varying from new roads across it to the improvement of Portoferraio's latrines.

He took over a building at the top of the town, between the two Medici fortresses, and converted it into the little Palazzo dei Mulini, where there is now an interesting museum. He also had the Villa San Martino, some five kilometres outside Portoferraio, but hardly ever stayed there. That, too, is open to visitors, but the furniture they are shown was not there in Napoleon's time. His death mask can be seen in the Church of the Misericordia, half-way up the hill to the Mulini, but there is not much else to remind one of the *Petit Caporal*, who liked to drive around his tiny kingdom accompanied by outriders in uniforms of green and red, with gold facings. All his decrees began with the words: 'Napoleon, Emperor, Sovereign of the Isle of Elba'. One of the books he left behind when he escaped to France had French on one page and English on the other. Its title? *The Hundred Thoughts of a Young Lady*.

The best of Elba's splendid beaches, in my opinion, are those of La Biodola on the north coast, Lacona and Marina di Campo in the south and, near the south-western corner, the three attractive little bays of Cavoli, Seccheto and Fetovaia. These have the whitest sand and wonderfully clear water. Marciana Marina, Porto Azzurro, Marina di Campo and, of course, Portoferraio are little fishing towns, with a life of their own, apart from the summer flood of visitors. High up on the mountainside are the charming little towns of Poggio, Marciana Alta, Sant' Ilario, San Piero, Rio nell' Elba and Capoliveri; the first two in particular were deliberately built in places that could not easily be reached – that was the only way in which the early Elbans could be fairly safe from the Barbary pirates.

The beaches, of course, have their disused plastic bottles, broken sandals and all the other muck that people throw into a sea they claim to love. But the ration is far smaller than that of the beaches of the '*continente*'. It would seem that the small tides of the Mediterranean move the flotsam and jetsam up or down the coast, but do not take much of it out to the islands. Elba's nicest months are May, June, September and even October. In each of those months I have swum far out to sea, thanking God for my incredible and undeserved good fortune.

About 40 kilometres inland from the Via Aurelia and the coast at Cecina, and 50 kilometres west of Siena, is a city which no visitor to Central Italy should fail to visit, Volterra. I have mentioned elsewhere that the Etruscans liked to build their towns high up on a ridge – so much so that, if one glances through the maps of cities in a guide book, one can often pick out those of Etruscan origin because they are long and narrow. Volterra, visible from many miles away, is a striking example of this custom; it stands more than 500 metres above sea level and on so precipitous a hill that part of the town has slid down into a deep valley. At the north-west end of the town there are spectacular and dangerous cliffs known as the *Balze*, where great stretches of Etruscan wall, as well as two churches, have disappeared in this way. This crumbling process has continued for centuries, for one of these churches was swept out of existence in 1140.

Many people – and I am one of them – find Volterra sad and sinister. A visit to the *Balze* helps to explain why. First, of course, is the constant menace of this erosion. Also, there is a wide waste space between the Etruscan wall and the town, which serves to remind one how much smaller Volterra is to-day than it used to be – the walls enclose roughly three times the acreage of the present built-up area. Lastly, what remains of these walls indicates how important was the civilisation that has disappeared. Some of the rectangular blocks of stone in the Etruscan wall at Volterra are enormous. According to George Dennis (*Cities and Cemeteries of Etruria*, London, 1848, re-printed by Dent), who made a very detailed examination of the fortifications in the 1840s, in one place, for a distance of over 40 metres, the wall is over 13 metres high, four metres thick and containing blocks that are three metres in length.

One of the city gates, the Porta all'Arco, is the most impressive Etruscan gate in existence. Here the original blocks of volcanic limestone of the door posts and of the internal walls between the inner and outer doorways stand out in contrast to the much smaller blocks with which the Romans repaired it in about 80 B.C. after it had been damaged during a siege by the Roman general, Sulla. The Romans put back above the outer arch the three great sculptured heads which some experts believe to have been the heads of three Etruscan gods, Tinia, Uni and Menrva. This Porta all'Arco very narrowly escaped destruction in the last war – the Germans had decided to pull it down in order to block the entrance to the Allies, but the people of Volterra protested so strongly that they were given 24 hours in which to think of an alternative course. They pulled up the flagstones of the steep street that leads down to the gate and completely blocked it.

Volterra's history in the Middle Ages is similar to that of most Italian cities, with disastrous wars between Guelfs and Ghibellines, between one rich family and another, between one city and another. There is even a near-repetition of the ruse employed in Perugia where Bishop Ercolano ordered a specially-fattened ox to be thrown over the walls to convince the hungry besiegers that the besieged were still living on the fat of the land. In Volterra, Bishop Justus, having miraculously increased the bread supply, ordered the people to throw a lot of it down to the besiegers, who gave up the siege and went despondently home. In 1361, Volterra surrendered to Florence and thereafter shared that city's successes and failures.

In almost every street in Volterra one hears the hum of machinery – electric lathes and chisels at work on the alabaster which provides the town's present wealth, and which is dug, in great greyish-white blocks out of caves in the valley of a small river called the Era. One variety is translucent and takes a fine polish, and another is much softer and rather brittle. The Etruscans worked alabaster, and there are several alabaster urns in the Etruscan museum, but the skill to use it seems then to have disappeared until the sixteenth century.

For many people, the Etruscan museum is Volterra's main attraction, and it is fascinating even for those who know nothing of Etruria beyond the name, for the carvings on many of the urns, perhaps 2,500 years old, are extraordinarily lively and realistic, with far more movement than the Greek sculpture of about the same period. (Since so much of the Etruscan work is based on Greek mythology, even the experts are not always prepared to say which is which.)

These urns are rectangular, and generally imitate houses (as do also some of the tombs in which the urns are found), presumably because the Etruscans believed it necessary to prolong the union between matter and spirit, between body and soul. Therefore the tombs were furnished with earthly possessions or their replicas, so that the deceased would be able to carry on as usual in the kingdom of the dead. And so that the dead person could easily be recognised in the next world, he or she was carved on the lid. In order to fit on the top of the urn, the body had to be much too small for the head. But the heads were extraordinarily true to life, if one can judge by the great variety of feature and expression. Other carvings round the sides of the urns often show the deceased person travelling to the next world on horseback, by boat, or in a covered waggon, not unlike those in which pioneers went westwards in America.

Those who are not very interested in urns may be interested in the Etruscan mirrors, small bronze figures and jewellery. In the room where are most of the bronzes, there is one that is so tall but so thin that it might easily escape notice. It is known as 'Shadow of the Evening' (*Ombra della Sera*), and indeed is very much like a man's shadow when the sun is very low. It must surely have provided the inspiration for a good deal of very modern sculpture, and especially for the elongated figures of Giacometti.

Apart from the Etruscan museum, which Dennis claimed to be 'more instructive than any other collection of Etruscan antiquities', Volterra has much to attract the visitor although the most common adjective to describe its architecture seems to be 'austere'. Certainly, it lacks the gentle influence of the Renaissance, and many of the buildings are made of large blocks of the depressingly yellow or brown local sandstone. The Palazzo de' Priori, finished in 1257, is said to be the oldest building of its kind in Tuscany: with its large wall spaces and small windows, it is more like a fortress than a town hall, although its coats of arms do something to conceal the severity and to give dignity to the piazza, which it shares with the Palazzo Pretorio. This building has an impressive tower, the Torre del Podestà, which is also called the Torre del Porcellino, or piglet, from the wild boar carved on the façade and from another boar on a bracket near the upper window of the tower. On market days, this piazza is as lively as any other piazza, but at other times I find it grim and sinister. Nor am I comforted when I walk down some street to the edge of the present city – before me lies a panorama of most unusual extent and lineal beauty, but the pale grey or yellow earth, so little relieved by green in winter or high summer, has something of lunar desolation about it.

Normally one leaves Volterra eastwards to Siena or westwards to Cecina and the coast. There is, however, a road that runs southwards to Massa Marittima, through that strange and little-known countryside marked *'Colline Metallifere'* on the maps. It well deserves its name for its soil contains alabaster, iron, sulphur, copper, lignite, lead, borax and other minerals. One is surprised, driving up hill and down dale through exceptionally wild country, suddenly to come across immense cooling chimneys, such as are used in the development of atomic energy, and great, metallic pipes spreading out in every direction. These chimneys are near a little town called Lardarello, which formerly produced boric acid exclusively for the production of glaze in the British pottery industry. The springs of volcanic gas are now used mainly for the production of electric power. Here and there in the forest, clouds of strongly sulphuric steam break through the surface of the soil, and the Romans knew the value of the mineral springs in this region for the cure of gout.

The principal reason for taking this difficult road is that, by mileage if not by time, it is the shortest way to get from Volterra to Massa Marittima, a charming hill town overlooking 17 kilometres of rich agricultural plain to Follonica and the sea. It is strange to think that, when Dennis was exploring this region for Etruscan ruins in the 1840s, this plain was so unhealthy that it was generally thought of as 'a desert seashore swamp, totally without interest, save as a reserve of wild boars and roebucks, without the picturesque, or antiquities, or good accommodation, or anything else to compensate for the fever-fraught atmosphere'. He assured his readers that 'from October to May it is as free from noxious vapours as any other part of Italy, and may be visited and explored with perfect impunity'. Malaria has long since been stamped out in this region, the Maremma, and the waste land has been turned into a land of prosperous farmers and passing tourists.

Massa Marittima's thirteenth-century cathedral is reached by a very wide flight of steps, which takes up one side of an almost triangular piazza. The admirable lions, the polygonal choir and several other features were the work of Giovanni Pisano in 1287. The other important buildings – the Palazzo Comunale and the Palazzo Pretoria – date from the same century, and make the piazza one of the most harmonious town centres I know. The cathedral, like the cathedral of Siena, was very much the creation of the people, for they even had to buy from their bishop the land on which it was to be built. Standing on the last outcrop of the *Colline Metallifere*, Massa Marittima has depended for its prosperity throughout the ages on the mining industry, and its Statute of Miners is said to be the oldest in Europe. And, as far as I know, it is one of only four Italian cities – the others being Borgo San Sepolcro, San Marino and Gubbio – where crossbow tournaments are still held.

Massa Marittima was once important enough to mint its own currency and to enlist its own mercenaries, but at different times it had to appeal to Pisa and Siena in its attempts to break the power of the barons, and these appeals led to a variation of the normal struggle between Guelfs and Ghibellines, or one family and another. The Sienese, settled in the upper part of the town, were frequently at daggers drawn with the Pisans, in the lower part. Several outbreaks of plague (attributed in one report to Siena to be the result of 'poison from the breath of snakes in Africa') reduced the population to 400 souls, and the town recovered its prosperity only in 1744, when Francis III, Grand Duke of Tuscany, brought in nearly 150 families from his native Lorraine.

Far away on the plain, the windscreen of a car caught the sunlight, as the tourists raced along the Via Aurelia, unaware of all the beauty and history in 'them thar hills'. Rather reluctantly, I joined them, and turned towards Rome. I had driven little more than 20 kilometres before a signpost to the right pulled me up with a jerk. 'Vetulonia – 5 kilometres' it announced.

I have already referred to George Dennis, whose *Cities and Cemeteries of Etruria* I find more fascinating than any more recent book I have read on the subject. Time after time in it he referred to the lost city of Vetulonia, one of the 12 cities of the original Etruscan Confederation, and so important that Rome adopted from it several of the insignia of officers of state, including the *fasces* – a bundle of scourging rods with an axe (which Mussolini later took over from the Romans). Its whereabouts had been discussed and disputed over by dozens of earlier Etruscologists, and Dennis thought he had discovered the real site, a few kilometres inland from Talamone, north of Orbetello. But even he put forward his claim only with diffidence, and here, nearly 40 kilometres farther north, was an ordinary signpost to Vetulonia. I felt almost as though I had myself made a discovery until I remembered that something like 140 years have gone by since Dennis had carried out his careful search.

With such ruined cities or cemeteries as Tarquinia, Cerveteri and Veii to be visited, the drive up to Vetulonia (Colonna until 1887, when the ancient name was resumed) is barely worth while, for the two or three carefully excavated tombs, like show houses on a building estate, are not very easy to find. There was a great variety of ways in which the Etruscans disposed of their dead, and the tombs I saw at Vetulonia were on two levels and covered over with an immense circular mound. The roof was made of layers of flat stones, with each row projecting beyond the row beneath it, thus making a domed roof. The view is magnificent – what view from what mountain-top in Tuscany is not? The plain below one, intersected by the Via Aurelia, was mosquito-poisoned swamp in Dennis's day and Vetulonia's coins, with anchors, tridents and dolphins, lead one to believe that this swamp was actually a sea inlet in the days of the Etruscans.

But almost every steep hill on the far side of the plain was once an Etruscan town or an Etruscan cemetery. More than 2,500 years ago, the men who hunted down there in the swamps or who grew emmer wheat on these steep hillsides be-longed to a civilisation that in many ways was much more ad-vanced than any other except that of Greece. In the intervening centuries, Greek and Latin have enabled knowledge to be passed on from one generation to another, from one country to an-other. And yet, of the Etruscan language our knowledge does not go much beyond the fact that it resembles no other known language.

From a distance, Monte Argentario appears to be another island which, indeed, it once was. It is an almost circular mountain, rising to well over 600 metres, with superb views of the coast, of the mainland mountains, and of Elba, Montecristo and the other islands of the Tuscan Archipelago. It is only within the last few years that its two little harbours, Porto Ercole to the south and Porto Santo Stefano to the north, have been 'discovered' but, being only 100 miles from Rome, builders are now busier there than in almost any other part of Italy. Inevitably little towns will soon be as crowded with expensive night-clubs, luxury hotels and so on as St Tropez or Juan-les-Pins. Already the film stars and the 'high life' of Rome's Via Veneto are spreading out to Monte Argentario's two islands, Giglio and Giannutri, and elegant yachts, most of them flying the flag of Panama to lessen taxation, are packed like sardines in the harbour of Santo Stefano.

Apart from their natural beauty, these two small fishing ports are excellent centres from which to explore some of the smaller Etruscan and ancient Roman towns. For Monte Argentario is not an island. Three strips of land (and two roads) connect it with the mainland, across a large, shallow lagoon. On the middle strip, and in the middle of the lagoon, stands Orbetello, a little walled town with a beautiful gate built by the Spaniards in 1557. (There are also the ruins of three Spanish forts at Porto Ercole.) And only some six miles away is the modern resort of Ansedonia, the elegant villas of which are probably built above the ruins of Cosa, which became a Roman colony in 273 B.C., but which was abandoned in the fourth century A.D.

Some 12 miles away to the north of Orbetello is the quiet and undeveloped little town of Talamone, with formidable walls, of which the lower part is Roman. Few guidebooks mention its existence, and yet it has had an extraordinary history. It is supposed to have been founded by Telamon, one of the Argonauts and king of Salamis, some 1300 years B.C. Later, it became an Etruscan city. In 225 B.C. the Romans, with Etruscans, Umbrians and others as allies – for they all had reasons to fear any invaders from the north – met at Talamone a large army of Gauls who were marching on Rome, and utterly defeated it. Two ruthless leaders landed here – Marius, uncle by marriage of Julius Caesar, who had been one of Rome's greatest generals and was elected consul for five periods in succession, but who left behind him a reputation for appalling brutality; and Barbarossa.

Turkish admiral and the greatest of the corsairs, who terrorised the inhabitants of seaside towns along most of the northern coast of the Mediterranean in the first half of the sixteenth century. (In Talamone he ordered the killing of the entire population except for one beautiful girl, Margherita, whom he took back to the harem of Suliman the Magnificent. She became the Sultan's favourite wife and had considerable political power.) Another unexpected visitor to Talamone was Garibaldi, who landed there in 1860, on his way from Genoa to Sicily in order to collect a few arms for his 1,000 ill-equipped legionaries.

And the population of this historic little town, according to my Garzanti Encyclopaedia, is 490!

For anybody interested in the Etruscans, as a holiday-maker rather than as an expert, Monte Argentario would be an ideal centre. Tarquinia, Saturnia, Viterbo, Bolsena, Vulci, Rusellae, Cerveteri and other Etruscan ruins are within easy reach by car, and a swim awaits the weary pilgrim on his return to Porto Santo Stefano or Porto Ercole. Few guidebooks even mention Pitigliano, and yet it is easily accessible from either Orbetello or Orvieto. The little town stands on a great cliff and is overshadowed by a great castle. Caves, rooms, perhaps whole houses, are dug out of the soft rock, not so much for reasons of poverty, as in Madera in the Italian deep south or in some towns in southern Spain, as for reasons of convenience – it is easier to make walls by digging inwards than by building outwards, especially since the hillside is so nearly precipitous. Many of the caves now used as store-rooms were originally Etruscan tombs.

The nearest approach I have seen to Pitigliano is the little French town of Rocamadour, in the Dordogne, but the castle there is a small affair in comparison with the Orsini castle, massive, but with Renaissance elegance, at Pitigliano. This, and the several other Orsini castles dotted about on local hill-tops, were inherited by that family after one of them had married an Aldobrandeschi heiress, Anastasia, in 1297, and this has some interest for Englishmen, for the first husband of Anastasia's mother had been Guy, son of Simon de Montfort, Earl of Leicester. I knew that Guy de Montfort, on his way back from one of the Crusades, had murdered the son of Richard of Cornwall, son of King John, in Viterbo, but I had not expected to find references to the family in this remote part of Tuscany. (Its remoteness is emphasised by the fact that several Pitigliano families are descended from Jews who settled there many centuries ago to escape from persecution.)

Four kilometres from Pitigliano is a village called Sovana (Soana in Roman times). It has its gate and its walls, and I was impressed by its church, with its immensely sturdy columns, but there is an air of poverty about the place greater than in any other place I have visited in Central Italy. This was the birth-place of Hildebrand, who became Gregory VII, one of the greatest of the popes. It was Gregory VII whose insistence that popes should take precedence over emperors compelled the Emperor Henry IV, in 1077, to take the humiliating 'road to Canossa' where he had to wait barefoot in the snow until the Pope, in Canossa castle near Reggio Emilia, agreed to grant him absolution. This poverty is all the more striking if one realises that Sovana was at one time the headquarters of the Aldobrandeschi family, and in the early years of the thirteenth century the Aldobrandeschi owned nearly the whole of the Maremma. They could boast – I imagine not quite accurately – that they had as many castles as there are days of the year.

Dennis, who must have been one of the earliest Etruscologists to visit Sovana – his name is still mentioned there with respect – wrote that there is 'a much larger number of cliff-hewn sepulchres than in any other Etruscan site, and a far greater variety of architectural decoration'. It was that sentence that took me there, but I should have found none of the tombs without a guide. I went there early one morning after a night of rain, and the owner of the smaller of the two bars led us, at a pace dictated by his enthusiasm, up hill and down dale, across fields and through chestnut forests to cave after cave hollowed out of the cliff. Many of them I should have dismissed as works of nature had our guide not been there to show us where Etruscan chisels had been at work to imitate houses, with pilasters, pediments, cornices and ceilings carved in obvious imitation of woodwork. 'Nowhere are the mouldings so singular and so varied', wrote Dennis, 'for they show the characteristics of widely remote countries and of very different ages. Egypt, Greece, Etruria and Rome have all their stamp here expressed.... It is better worth a pilgrimage than one half of known Etruscan sites.' So much has been discovered at other Etruscan sites since Dennis's time that Sovana no longer justifies such praise. Indeed two of the best-known books on the Etruscans make no reference to the place at all. But I liked it all the better for that reason – at the cost of a tip to a guide, a tourist as ignorant as I am of Etruscan art and archaeology was able to realise a little of the excitement that must be felt by the expert when he undertakes a new 'dig'.

To learn more about the Etruscans and their way of life, however, one should go to Tarquinia, the first frescoed tombs of which were discovered in the seventeenth century. These tombs, to be visited with a guide, are at some distance from the present town, and also – as in the case of most Etruscan cemeteries – quite a long way from the original Etruscan city, of which only a few ruins now remain. More and more tombs have been discovered and their treasures removed – some by the great museums but a great number by '*tombaroli*', robbers who use the most modern scientific implements to discover which tombs are best worth breaking into at night. And the effect of fresh air on ancient paintings from which fresh air had been excluded for more than two thousand years has, of course, been disastrous. Nevertheless, the tombs of Tarquinia are immensely interesting, and teach one a great deal about this mysterious people.

One sees, for example, that Etruscan women had far more freedom than did Greeks or Romans. Their presence at banquets and their very widespread use of perfumes and jewels led many Roman writers to class them as whores, despite the num-

12   *Florence: the Duomo, from the campanile*

ber of Etruscan sarcophagi and urns portraying husbands and wives lounging amicably side by side. The Etruscans were very clever workers of gold and other metals. Their dentists were adept at crowning and bridging teeth with gold, and one of the more interesting but less attractive exhibits in the Tarquinia museum is a set of false teeth. They were very fond of animals, and seem to have been the first people in Italy to make impressive military use of horses – a famous terracotta in the museum is the pair of winged horses that formed part of the pediment of a local temple. They are amazingly lifelike. I have suggested elsewhere that sculptors of today have probably turned to the Etruscans for inspiration (as Michelangelo and Donatello, to mention only two artists of the Renaissance, are believed to have done). They could hardly do better for, whereas the Greeks sought to reproduce perfect men and women, the Etruscans reproduced human beings as they are, with all their faults and failings. Indeed, as Michael Grant (*The Ancient Mediterranean*, Weidenfeld, London, 1969) points out, they went even further – they showed 'a special taste for parody and the grotesque.... Etruscan sculpture, for example, showed little concern for ideal abstractions or refinements, but infused its realism with a touch of exaggeration in order to make a vivid, lifelike impression'. I suppose it is for that very reason that I find the sculptures on their tombs and sarcophagi so much more fascinating than the pure perfection of Greek statues.

13 Florence: the Ponte Vecchio

5. San Gimignano and Siena

The town of San Gimignano has a population of about 7,000. It has works of art by Jacopo della Quercia, Donatello, Benozzo Gozzoli, Ghirlandaio, Filippino Lippi, Pinturicchio, and other famous artists that would sell at Sothebys for immense sums. It is one of the most unchanged mediaeval towns in Italy. And I should guess that the world's tourist offices display more posters of it than of any other Italian town, except possibly Florence and Rome. It would deserve much of this fame even if it had not, like Pisa with its Leaning Tower, one feature that is unique. No other town has a similar collection of mediaeval towers. You see them in the distance as you drive from Florence to Rome along the Via Cassia; and you will be singularly pressed for time or singularly lacking in healthy curiosity if you do not turn off between the olive orchards to get a closer view.

Indeed, you would do well to turn off long before you see the towers of San Gimignano for between Florence and Siena is the Chiantigiana, the region which produces the best-known wine of Italy. The very best Chianti is not necessarily to be found in those attractive round flasks covered with straw. Indeed, much of the wine in such flasks probably does not come from the region south of Florence which is known as the Chiantigiana, and there is a feud between the makers of 'Chianti classico', to be distinguished by the label with a black cock on the flask, and the other officially recognised Chianti, the label of which represents a *putto*, one of those small angels one sees floating above the Holy Family in so many religious paintings. In the former case, the emphasis is on the relatively small region in which the wine is made; in the other, it is on the varieties of the grapes that are used. (Chianti does not deserve the name unless it includes Sangiovese, Trebbiano and Malvasi grapes.) This rivalry is forgotten only when some outsider seeks to use the name.

But I recommend the Chiantigiana to you not only on account of its wine, although I can think of few more peaceful and pleasant activities than to visit Sant' Andrea in Percussina, near San Casciano, and to drink wine at the inn where Macchiavelli, in exile from Florence, drank and gambled and wrote his books some five centuries ago. Drink it as he would have done – with mouthfuls of garlic bread dipped in olive oil. I recommend this region because its scenery is so typical of Tuscany – great, forest-covered hills, magnificent avenues of cypresses leading up to villas that were built at the time of the Medici, neat rows of vines and vast orchards of olives, flourishing in pale brown, stony soil in which, one would think, few plants could survive – until, quite suddenly, the flowers come out in that brief season between the cold winter and the long, dry, hot summer. To me, the Chiantigiana is more 'Italian' than any other part of Italy.

In many Tuscan towns you see big, square buildings which can easily be identified as truncated towers, reminders in stone or brick of the appalling wars between the great, aristocratic families. As with most other wars, a greater loyalty was paraded to conceal a less worthy ambition – in the case of the Italians, loyalty to Pope or Emperor, to the Guelfs or the Ghibellines was the excuse for a bloodthirsty struggle for family advancement. I have pointed out elsewhere that, as the merchants won influence in the cities, they managed to destroy many of the castles from which the robber barons took their cut on passing traffic and to compel them to live inside the walls, where they could be kept under some measure of control. This meant, however, that although family feuds were more circumscribed they were more intense. The *palazzi* within the walls became more and more like fortresses, and each family wanted to have a higher tower than his neighbour, partly for purposes of defence and partly to keep up with the Joneses. Many of these towers were hurriedly and badly built. Some of them collapsed in the winter gales. The most obvious form of control was to insist that no privately owned tower should be taller than the tower of the Palazzo Pubblico or some other public building. Finally, most of them were taken down.

More than a dozen of San Gimignano's 60 or 70 towers are still standing, and in this respect this small town is unique. Its nearest rival is Bologna, with only three – although the Torre Asinelli there is remarkable in that it is only 46 feet lower than the cross on the dome of London's St Paul's and it leans an alarming four feet out of the perpendicular. In another respect, the people of San Gimignano were almost unique for, in 1353, they became so sickened by the costly and stupid fighting between their local Guelfs and Ghibellines that they sent a parchment to Florence, asking to be taken over and leaving a blank space in which the Florentines were to put down their terms. It is pleasant to record that Florence, in reply, returned this document with the request that San Gimignano should state its own terms of submission. Had the Sangiminesi not had the good sense to realise that they needed the protection of a larger power, it is very doubtful whether their town would have retained its mediaeval appearance to the present day.

One more fact about this little town is unusual – the local saint, Santa Fina, was only 15 years old when she died. At the eastern end of the south aisle of the Cathedral is a special chapel in her honour, decorated in part by frescoes which were Ghirlandaio's first work. There was not much he could record about her short life – at the age of ten, when she went to fetch water from the fountain, a young man gave her an orange, whereupon she had such a lecture from her mother about the danger of accepting gifts from strange young men that her ignorance seemed to her to be a major sin, which she could expiate only by lying down on a plank for the remaining five years of her life. A more prosaic version is that the poor girl was paralysed. Whatever the cause of her immobility, she did so many good deeds that, on the day of her death, all the church bells tolled of their own accord, and the plank on which she had lain was covered with violets, the sweet scent of which spread throughout the town. The yellow violets that grow out from the interstices of the towers are supposed first to have blossomed during her funeral.

San Gimignano has two important squares, the corner of one meeting the corner of the other, and it is difficult to say which is the more beautiful. The Piazza del Duomo has the finer buildings – the Duomo, the Palazzo Comunale and the Palazzo del Podestà – but the Piazza della Cisterna, with its octagonal fourteenth century well in the middle, its surrounding houses of the same period and its floor of old bricks in herring-bone pattern, gives one a better impression of what life was like in a mediaeval town. It is less grand and more informal. One can more easily imagine the local shop-keepers, grouped round the well and discussing the disputes between the leading families and the latest tower one or other of them was building. In the case of San Gimignano, the tower of the Palazzo Comunale was the one the height of which nobody must exceed. The view from the top of it, I am assured, is well worth the effort of climbing it.

To me, nothing in San Gimignano is more attractive than the courtyard of the Palazzo Comunale. The outside staircase, with a right-angle turn half-way up it, leads to an unusually elegant loggia. Old brick paving and an old well add to its charm. Dante must have walked up these stairs when he came as Florentine ambassador in 1300 to urge the priors, meeting in the Sala del Consiglio, to join the (Guelf) Tuscan League. (I have already recorded the fact that, 53 years later, the Sangiminesi surrendered themselves to Florence on any terms the Florentines chose to dictate.)

Adjoining the Palazzo Comunale is the Duomo, also known as

La Collegiata, with a modern façade, but a fine flight of steps leading up to its very interesting interior. The north wall has two rows of frescoes of Old Testament subjects, starting at the top with the creation of Adam by three rays of light passing from the mouth of Christ. (This cathedral is one of several in Italy in which a coin in a slot will turn on the lights, and give you both a much better view and looks of gratitude from other visitors with a stricter sense of economy.) Other unusual frescoes in this series show Noah herding the animals into the Ark and the Israelites crossing the Red Sea, with the women wearing smart mediaeval costumes and riding camels. At the west end of the Duomo there is a large fresco of the Last Judgment by another Sienese artist, Taddeo di Bartolo, with a particularly gruesome picture of life in Hell, and the way some of the devils are treating some of the poor naked sinners possibly justifies the fact that it is too high up for the details to be easily distinguished.

In another church, Sant'Agostino, there are 17 scenes by Benozzo Gozzoli, from the life of St Augustine, the first 13 of which are based on the saint's *Confessions*. The same artist in the same church painted a picture in which Christ and the Virgin are on their knees, pleading to God the Father to check the plan of some angels to shoot plague-impregnated arrows at human beings.

There are several other important churches but, of all towns in Italy, there must be few in which the visitor so wants to be out in the streets, trying to picture himself as a citizen some six centuries ago.

Sometime in 1920 I arrived at Siena by a late evening train from Rome. I was then Rome correspondent of *The Times*, and I was on some mission to do with 'news', although the Sienese, so often at war in mediaeval times, have sensibly kept out of the headlines in recent centuries. What my mission was I can no longer remember, but I do remember coming out of some dark and narrow street into that magnificent square, the Piazza del

Campo. There was enough of a moon to light up the houses that form a semicircle round it, and the wonderful façade of the Palazzo Pubblico with the 101 metres of the Torre del Mangia (St Paul's Cathedral, London, 111 metres), but not enough to show up the few indications of modernity. It was a cold, clear night, I remember, and I had the huge place to myself; I had stepped back six centuries into a dead but beautiful world. It is partly to preserve that memory that, although I live less than 70 miles from Siena, I have never gone there on any 2 July or 16 August, when the Campo is so crowded with spectators of the *Palio* that the photographs suggest there would not have been room for me even if I had gone.

For some reason that escapes me, unless it be that on the eve of the Battle of Montaperti in 1260, the keys of the city were placed on an altar as a gift to the Virgin Mary 'for ever so long as the world endures', the horse races known as the *Palio* are held in her honour, and the horse representing each of the ten competing *contrade* is taken into the parish church to be blessed before the races begin. (There are seventeen *contrade*, and their emblems are astonishingly varied, including a lion, a goose, an owl, a dragon, a unicorn, a caterpillar, a tortoise, a giraffe, a wolf, and a porcupine.) The names are derived from the decorated cart that was used by the bull-fighters of each *contrada* before the Palio was introduced in 1659.

Siena's emblem is similar to that of Rome – the wolf suckling the twins – and this fact is held to justify the claim of the Sienese that their city was founded by Senus, son of Remus, who fled northwards after Romulus had murdered his father. It did not play much of a part in history, however, until the twelfth century, after Milanese refugees from the Emperor Frederick Barbarossa had emigrated there, bringing with them their experience of the wool trade. In the thirteenth and fourteenth centuries, this town, with none of the geographical advantages of Florence, was nevertheless a serious rival, both in the wool trade and in banking. One member of the Chigi family was said to own a hundred ships and to have a hundred branches of his bank, and to this day one of Italy's most important banks is the *Monte dei Paschi di Siena*, a name which suggests its early links with the wool trade. For a very brief time after 1260, Siena was even stronger militarily than Florence. The battle of Montaperti, in September of that year, was one of the most remarkable battles in Italian history, and it deserves a paragraph because it illustrates the passionate and determined side of the Sienese character – its motto *'Cor magis tibi Sena pandit'* (Sienna opens its heart more widely to you) reminds you of the other side, a friendliness which adds to the city's attractions.

In 1260, Siena was threatened not by the Florentines alone – and it is alleged that there were 40,000 of them! – but also by troops from Perugia, Lucca, Bologna, San Gimignano, Volterra, Prato and other city states. Faced by an ultimatum threatening destruction if they did not surrender both their city and the Ghibelline emigrants from Florence who had found refuge in it, some of the local authorities wanted to give way. And no wonder; to meet this army, there were only the men of Siena, some 500 Florentine refugees, and 800 German mercenaries sent by Manfred, son of the late Emperor Frederick II. But the defeatists were outvoted. The Council, which in those days met in the church of San Cristoforo, gave the envoys from Florence a defiant reply, and the bells rang to call the citizens to arms. A leader, with the well-omened name of Buonaguida, was chosen, and he led a procession to the Duomo where, kneeling with the bishop at the altar, he handed over the keys of all the city's gates to the keeping of the Virgin. His gesture was followed by a rousing speech by the bishop himself. (This ceremony is interesting, since the Ghibellines, who were traditionally supporters of the Holy Roman Emperor, were going out to fight the Guelfs, who were traditionally supporters of the Pope.)

Next day the two armies clashed at Montaperti a few miles outside the city. In the Via della Città is the Palazzo Chigi-Saracini, and from its tower, then much higher than it is today, a certain Cerreto Ceccolini called out details of the battle. His running commentary ended with the cry: 'Their banners fall.

They are broken! They are broken!' In fact, the disaster for Florence was complete, for the Sienese captured their *carroccio*, the chariot with its altar and other religious or national emblems, round which mediaeval armies fought, as soldiers in later centuries fought round the regimental standard. Florence could have suffered no greater humiliation. A bare 30 years earlier they had shown their contempt for the Sienese by catapulting dead donkeys and manure over city walls, and now a donkey dragged the standard of Florence through the dust.

The Sienese who never missed an opportunity for a public celebration have had no other moment in their history that so justified one. Nevertheless, Lilian Notestein (*Hill Towns of Italy*, Hutchinson, 1963) mentions two such opportunities that help to reveal their character. In 1311, their first great artist, Duccio di Buoninsegna, finished, after three years, an elaborate altar piece for the Duomo. Bells rang in all the churches, there was a public holiday, and the altar piece was carried in a great procession, led by the bishop and all the local authorities, carrying lighted candles and accompanied by drummers and trumpeters, from Duccio's studio to the Duomo. Where else and in what period would a painting be given such a welcome? A second celebration mentioned by Lilian Notestein was justified by the first day – 1 June 1343 – on which water, brought by pipeline from some fifteen miles away, first flowed into a fountain in the Campo.

A fountain, not *the* fountain that decorates the Campo today, nor even the fountain of which the present one is a copy. The first fountain, which was given the name of *Fonte Gaia* because the arrival of water was the excuse for gay celebrations that lasted more than a week, was not a very grand affair. It was surmounted by a fine Greek or Roman statue (signed by Lysippus) that had been found while workmen were digging the foundations of some palace, but Siena entered a bad period and, after fourteen years of defeat and disaster, someone put the blame on this pagan statue. The fickle crowd smashed it to pieces which, typically, they buried in Florentine soil. It was not until 1419 that Siena's greatest sculptor, Jacopo della Quercia, finished the fountain of which the present one is a nineteenth-century copy – the original, which had suffered considerably in the intervening centuries, can be seen in the Palazzo Pubblico.

The present copy may fall far short of its very beautiful original, but it is good enough for me since it stands, where Jacopo's fountain stood, in one of the most beautiful squares in the world. The Campo is shell-shaped, with the semi-circular edge facing downhill towards the hinge, which is the entrance to the Palazzo Pubblico. From this central point nine narrow strips of travertine radiate out across the piazza, to remind the Sienese that they used to be governed by a Council of Nine, and the intervening segments are paved, herring-bone fashion, with old pink bricks. The Fonte Gaia is near the outer rim and facing the Palazzo Pubblico. (Most guidebooks place it in the centre of the piazza; it would not be nearly so effective if it were.)

The Campo was, of course, the place where the people met in times of crisis or celebrations. When the great bell at the top of the Mangia tower rang out in warning, a candle was lit at the entrance to the Palazzo Pubblico, and Siena's soldiers were expected to be on parade before it burnt out. There used to be chains which could be fixed across the entry of every street into the piazza to exclude knights on horseback in times of local disorder. Boccaccio, in his life of Dante, describes how, on one occasion, the poet stood there for hours, so engrossed in a book he had just bought that he seemed to be unaware of a tournament that was in progress, with the noisy accompaniment of trumpeters and yelling crowds, 'yet there was never one that saw him stir thence, nor once raise his eyes from the book'.

The Palazzo Pubblico was built between 1289 and 1309, with another storey and the two wings added, to its great advantage, in 1711. The Mangia Tower, named after a very popular local character whose task it had been to strike the hours, was finished in 1345. The little chapel at its foot was built in 1352, in thanksgiving for the end of the Black Death which, in four years, reduced the population by about 30,000. And high up on the façade of the Palazzo is a large circle with the letters 'IHS' (*Iesu Hominum Salvator*) in its centre – this was placed there at the instigation of San Bernardino, instead of the coats of arms one finds fixed to most Italian city halls, because, he claimed, these coats of arms served to perpetuate rivalry between the great ruling families. (Undoubtedly they did, but they add a lot to the attractiveness of these buildings today.)

I have already mentioned that, in order to check the propensities of these families to interfere with trade it was often found necessary to destroy the castles from which they carried out their forays, and to insist that at least one member of the family should live within the city walls, despite the encouragement thus given to street fighting and the excessive use of the dagger in dark streets at night. (The Rialto Bridge in Venice used to have a drawbridge in the middle, partly to allow the passage of larger ships, but also to prevent the Nicoletti family on one side of the canal and the Castellani family on the other side from coming to blows.) This rivalry was possibly even worse in Siena than in most other mediaeval Italian cities because the families had been powerful for a longer period – the Tolomei, whose fights with the Salimbeni led to many decades of disturbances, claimed to trace their ancestry back to the Ptolomies in Egypt. But this concentration of rivalries within the city walls has left a beneficial legacy, in that such streets as the Via di Città and the Via Banchi di Sopra have, perhaps, more beautiful mediaeval palaces than any other city in Italy.

Siena's triumph over Florence at Montaperti was short-lived. The pope's candidate for the throne of Sicily, Charles d'Anjou, defeated Manfred at Benevento, in southern Italy, and this amounted to a Guelf victory over the Ghibellines throughout the country. Nine years after Montaperti, the Florentines crushed the Sienese army at Colle d'Elsa, twenty kilometres north of Siena. Nevertheless, it was during the following eighty years that the city achieved its greatest fame, mainly under the government of the Council of Nine, which represented the best of the merchant class and the members of which changed every two months. It was during that period that both the Palazzo Pubblico and the Duomo were built. Then, after a lapse of a century, there was a short revival of glory under the influence of Pope Pius II, who considered himself a Sienese, although he was not born there. In the sixteenth century, after almost two years of siege by French, Spanish, Swiss and Florentine troops, Siena had to surrender to Duke Cosimo de' Medici who was himself under the ultimate control of the Holy Roman Emperor. The Sienese of today are amongst the most cheerful and friendly Italians, but nobody would suggest that they love the Florentines.

Once one is inside the Palazzo Pubblico, its turbulent history is largely forgotten. There are dungeons, of course, and paintings of war and of warriors (most notably a splendid portrait of a condottiere general, Guidoriccio da Fogliana, by Simone Martini), but there is also his *Maestà*, in which the Madonna, very aristocratic and richly dressed for a mother whose child was born in a stable, admirably illustrates the reluctance of Sienese artists to face the grimmer realities of life. And, in the Sala della Pace, there are the famous frescoes by Ambrogio Lorenzetti, which I find very attractive, not only because *The Effects of Good Government* tells one so much about the life of Siena and its countryside in his day, but also because there is so much more vigour and vitality than in the work of his predecessors and his contemporaries.

The Duomo is always referred to in such phrases as 'one of the finest examples of Italian Gothic architecture'. (It would perhaps be more accurate to call it Romanesque with Gothic additions.) I am very unfortunate in that I cannot appreciate it or its nearly-related cathedral in Orvieto. I miss the soaring aspiration of French Gothic, and I find the exteriors of both churches fussy. In Siena, the cupola is so nearly hidden by the frills of the façade that it seems unnecessary, and the horizontal stripes of green and white marble of the tower so distract attention that one may easily fail to appreciate its proportions.

It is a striking example of the custom in many towers, especially in Tuscany, of increasing the number of its windows as it gains height. Presumably, this means that each storey is lighter than the one below it, since it uses fewer bricks, but it may at first give a contrary impression. The tower in Siena has six tiers, of which the lowest has only one window and the uppermost one has six.

These very superficial impressions are undoubtedly heightened by the austere and stately palaces one passes as one climbs up the hill from the Campo to the Duomo. It is difficult to believe that the Duomo is older than several of them and of approximately the same age as the Palazzo Pubblico. Few churches have so involved the whole population in their construction – the marble was a charge on the rates and every Sienese who owned an ox or an ass was expected to fetch two loads of marble a year from the quarry. The building was begun probably in 1229, but the façade was not finished at the end of the century, by which time Arnolfo di Cambio had begun to build the Duomo in Florence. The fear that Florence would have a bigger and better cathedral undoubtedly influenced the Sienese to take an extraordinary decision – their existing Duomo, large though it was, should be only the transept for an even larger one. Work on this project began in 1340, and its ruins on the south side of the present building give some idea of the ambitious plan; if completed, it would have given Siena one of the largest temples in the world. But, as already recorded, in 1348 came the Black Death. By the time it had passed, Siena had neither the money nor the will to build the new cathedral. Instead, the existing one was completed, with its façade of red, black and white marble and its multitude of sculptured figures, the general plan of which is attributed to Giovanni Pisano (although he was dead long before it was completed).

The three most impressive features of the Duomo are the pavement, the pulpit and the so-called Libreria, opening out of the north aisle. The pavement, indeed, is unique. It consists of a large number of allegorical designs, many from Old Testament stories, drawn by more than forty eminent artists and worked out in coloured marbles or in a kind of *graffito* work in which lines of varying depth and emphasis were scratched on white marble and then filled in with black or coloured stucco. These pavements date from the middle of the thirteenth to the middle of the fourteenth century, and many of them are so badly worn that they have to be covered over or roped off for most of the year.

The pulpit, octagonal in shape, is of white marble, standing on eight granite columns. It is the second of the four pulpits ascribed to the Pisano family. The first, by Niccolà alone, is in the Baptistery in Pisa, and was completed in 1260. The second is this Siena pulpit, for which Niccolà had the help of his son, Giovanni, and other young artists, and it was carved between 1265 and 1269. The third, by Giovanni alone, is in the church of Sant'Andrea in Pistoia. The last, also the work of Giovanni, made between 1302 and 1310, is the pulpit in the cathedral at Pisa. Of these, the Siena pulpit is the least classical and the most romantic.

The Libreria was built in 1495 at the instigation of Pope Pius III, to extol the greatness of his Piccolomini uncle, Pius II, and it is remarkable for the ten frescoes in which Pinturicchio described the life of this outstanding pope. They are a tribute rather to the artist's ability and imagination than to his respect for historical accuracy. Tactfully, he makes no reference to the pope's dissolute life before he decided to become a priest; regrettably, there is no fresco showing Pius condemning Sigismondo Malatesta of Rimini as the worst scoundrel 'of all men who have ever lived or ever will live'. One of the frescoes, however, shows Pius, after he had been shipwrecked, being received by an old, white-haired man in brown, surrounded by courtiers in elegant Renaissance garments. The old man, we are told, is James I of Scotland who, in fact, died when he was 43, and the scenic background to this Scottish meeting could not possibly be found anywhere north of the Alps.

Vasari claimed that some of the work on these frescoes was

done by Raphael, but most experts doubt this, although the young man in the lower part of the fresco of St Catherine's canonisation is generally held to be a portrait of him; the man at his side is almost certainly Pinturicchio himself. It is sometimes argued that the frescoes are merely decorative and lack all spiritual significance. This may be so, but the colour and detail are so glorious that they should surely rank among the major artistic attractions of Italy.

Behind and below the Duomo, reached down a long and steep flight of steps, is the Baptistery with a remarkable hexagonal marble font designed by Siena's most famous sculptor, Jacopo della Quercia. Round it are statuettes (two by Donatello) alternating with five bronze panels in bas-relief (of which one is by della Quercia, one by Lorenzo Ghiberti and one by Donatello). In the valley between this Baptistery and the large and prominent church of San Domenico (with two frescoes of the life of St Catherine, a portrait of her by Andrea Vanni, and her preserved head) is the house in which she lived.

Catherine was the twenty-fourth of 25 children of a dyer who, fortunately, was fairly wealthy. She took the veil at the age of eight. When she was 20 she had a vision, the ensuing ecstasy of which nearly killed her, of a mystical marriage with Christ. Her early home life must have been difficult. She turned her bedroom into a cell with a stone as her pillow and she seldom spoke to anybody except her confessor. Nevertheless, she developed an extraordinary political influence. Outspoken and humorous, she carried on a correspondence with many of the world leaders of the fourteenth century, and she went to Avignon, where she persuaded Pope Gregory XI to end the 70 years of papal exile in France and to return to Rome. In a letter to his excitable successor, Urban VI, she wrote: 'For the sake of your crucified Lord, keep those hasty movements of yours a little in check.' (This he failed to do, and he died, deserted and despised.) St Catherine died in 1380, at the age of 33. Her house is now a series of small chapels or oratories and has little to help one to understand this extraordinary woman.

One should, if possible, visit the *Pinacoteca Nazionale*, as important to those interested in the characteristics of Sienese art as the gallery in Perugia is important to students of the Umbrian school. All the great Sienese painters from the twelfth to the sixteenth century are represented. One is delighted by the colour, the details of the countryside (however unseasonable some of the flowers may be), the way in which everything is a little more vivid than life. 'Steeped in a religious mysticism that must have rendered shocking to them the humanistic portrayal of saints, they kept their madonnas strictly in an unearthly land' (Hubbard Hutchinson, *From Rome to Florence*, Putnam, New York and London).

A small and irrelevant footnote. One church in Siena that normally escapes notice is the small early Renaissance church of Santa Maria delle Neve, where there is an altar-piece showing the Virgin accompanied by saints and angels who carry snowballs. According to legend, the Madonna appeared before the fourth century pope, Liberius, one night in August, and told him to build a church wherever he should find snow on the ground next morning. Which, miraculously, he did. This was the origin of Santa Maria Maggiore in Rome and, presumably, of this little church in Siena.

14   Arezzo: the church of Santa Maria della Pieve

6. Siena to Viterbo

Twenty-six kilometres down the road from Siena to Rome is the little town of Buonconvento, chiefly famous for the fact that the Emperor, Henry VII, died there in 1313. His father had been an impoverished Count of Luxemburg, before iron smelting and international organisations had brought prosperity to that tiny country, and his poverty greatly hampered his prospects as Holy Roman Emperor. In the hope of increasing his income and his prestige, he marched into Italy, failed in a half-hearted attempt to capture Florence, found Rome already occupied by his chief rival, King Robert of Naples, and thus failed to get himself crowned Emperor by the Pope in St Peter's. He had started with the support of the Ghibellines and of dissident Guelfs such as Dante, who wanted to restore the authority of the emperors against the popes. But an emperor without cash and courage stood small chance of success. He died at Buonconvento while he was planning to make a fresh attack on Rome, and, as I reported in an earlier chapter, he is buried in the Duomo of Pisa. His much more pugnacious son, King John of Bohemia, died 33 years later on the battlefield of Crécy.

Buonconvento really comes into this book only because it is here that a road branches off to Monte Oliveto Maggiore, with its immense and impressive Benedictine monastery, in its oasis of cypresses surrounded by an impoverished and hilly desert. One of the occupations of the six monks of the Olivetan Order who still live there is the restoration of ancient books – which they do probably more efficiently than anyone else in the world. Brother Placido, who directs the work, is very patient towards enquirers who are genuinely interested. Many of the most valuable old books that were badly damaged during the 1966 floods in Florence have been restored here.

But the monastery is more widely known for another reason. Its Great Cloister contains frescoes of the life of St Benedict by two major painters of the Late Renaissance, Luca Signorelli and Il Sodoma. Of the 36 paintings, only eight are by Signorelli, and they are very original both in treatment and in subject. His muscular and vigorous figures, made almost three-dimensional by a startling use of white paint, help to explain why they had so great an influence on the young Michelangelo (who was only 22 when these frescoes were painted).

Since his subject was the life of the saint, he was able to break away from the usual biblical stories or groupings of worshippers round the Madonna and Child. Even so, his choice was unexpected. For example, he shows Totila, king of the Ostrogoths, who twice captured Rome in the sixth century, and who abandoned his plan on the second occasion utterly to destroy the city because his chief enemy, Belisarius, wrote him a letter to remind him that Rome was 'the greatest and most notable of all cities scattered under the sun', and that, in destroying it, 'thou wilt destroy not what is another's, but thine own'. He ended with the reminder that 'as his deeds are, such is the name by which a king will live'. Totila not only did not destroy Rome; he ordered the restoration of some of the buildings his army had damaged during the first occupation. Signorelli shows this proud general on his knees before St Benedict. Another unexpected painting shows a workman being thrown by Satan from a high wall and being brought back to life by the saint. Yet another shows the saint refusing to be taken in by a soldier in an attractive but unconvincing disguise.

As far as Il Sodoma is concerned, these frescoes were his first major work. I shall remember them less for their portrayal of people and events than for the exquisite scenery in the background, astonishingly reminiscent of Chinese landscape paintings. In the third fresco of the series, he painted an interesting self-portrait – the young man with long hair, looking towards the observer as though he were explaining the activities around him. The monastery was founded in 1319 by a member of the Tolomei family, whose conflicts with the Salimbeni had caused so much bloodshed in Siena.

Sixteen kilometres south of Buonconvento, there is a turning off to the left. It is worth taking, for two reasons – if time presses, it will take you to the *autostrada* at Chiusi, and it will take you past the two very attractive little towns of Pienza and Montepulciano.

'Unique' is a dangerous word to use, but it can safely be used about Pienza, for all the buildings round its small central piazza were built by one architect, Bernardo Rossellino, between 1459 and 1462. The visitor finds himself suddenly surrounded by the Early Renaissance. The largest building, with a charming well in front of it, is the Palazzo Piccolomini, copied from the 'rustica' style of the Palazzo Rucellai in Florence, with its huge blocks of roughly-hewn stone that, in their turn, were obviously copied from the walls of the Etruscans. Opposite this *palazzo* is the Bishop's Palace. Between the two, on the left, is the Palazzo Pubblico, with an attractive colonnade and tower. And, facing this building, is the Duomo, with a simple and dignified façade and a bright, Gothic interior. A strange painting, by Vecchietta, shows an Assumption, attended by the Sicilian saint, Agatha, holding a salver containing her breasts, cut off by her torturers. This *motif* is not so unusual as one might expect, and the resemblance of the breasts to bells led to the adoption of St Agatha as patron saint of bell-founders.

What is the history of this strange little town? Until the fifteenth century it was called Corsignano, and its one notable citizen was Aeneas Silvio Piccolomini, who became Pope Pius II and in whose honour Pinturicchio painted his ten frescoes in Siena Cathedral. His coat of arms appears on or inside each of the buildings on the piazza. This was the pope who so vehemently condemned Sigismondo Malatesta, who rebuilt a church at Rimini and filled it with his own coat of arms or initials and those of his mistress, Isotta. After he had become pope, Pius, in his early 50s, returned to Corsignano with a suite of six cardinals and 100 knights (several of whose houses add to the attractions of the present town) and set about the transformation of Corsignano into Pienza. The ubiquity of his coat of arms, the claim that his family could trace its descent back to Romulus, and the very blatant opportunism that characterised his career indicate an absence of Christ-like humility, but he was a man of great intelligence, wit and learning. He died two years after Pienza had been completed, while he was organising a crusade against the Turks, since when this 'made' town has lived on, as nearly oblivious of the modern world as a town on a main road can be. Its piazza may lack the warmth and friendliness of so many Italian squares; architecturally, it is perfect.

Montepulciano, by any standard, must rank among the most attractive hill-towns of Tuscany. You enter it through an imposing gate in the fourteenth-century walls and are almost at once reminded that the town was ruled by Florence, by a column on the top of which is the heraldic lion of that city, *il Marzocco*, a copy of which stands outside the Palazzo Vecchio. Should you intend to stay in Montepulciano, watch out very carefully for that lion, for within a few yards of it is (as far as I discovered) the only hotel in the town and, should you miss it, you must continue up the steep and narrow main street for about a kilometre before you find a road which will take you down the hill again, and enable you to turn back, outside the walls, to the gate by which you came in.

It is certainly not a town in which to drive, partly because the street is so narrow, but mainly because you cannot then see the fine Renaissance palaces that flank it. Three of them were built by Antonio di Sangallo, who had been sent by Florence in 1512 to build Montepulciano's fortifications, and at least two by Vignola, who collaborated with Michelangelo in the construction of St Peter's in Rome. This long street leads in the end to the Piazza Grande, with a Palazzo Comunale which reminds one of the Palazzo Vecchio in Florence, a beautiful well, the cathedral with an unfinished façade, and, opposite it, the imposing Renaissance Palazzo Nobili-Tarugi. I must admit that I was slightly disappointed by this Piazza Grande, partly because the frequent direction signs to the *Centro Storico* had raised my hopes so high, partly because I was tired before I even began the long uphill walk to it, but above all because a number of young men on the loudest motor cycles I have ever heard used this narrow main street and the road outside the walls back to the main gate as a speed track with human obstacles. But on a clear day the view from the tower of the Palazzo Comunale must be almost un-equalled – eastwards, over the plain of the Chiana and Lake Trasimeno to Cortona, Perugia and the main ranges of the Apennines, westwards to Siena and the Colle Metallifere, southwards to Monte Amiata, more than 1,700 metres high and often capped with snow while the intervening hills, with their olives and their cypresses, are bathed in sunshine. One would love Montepulciano, even if it did not produce some of the best wine in Italy.

Just outside Montepulciano, and three or four hundred metres off the road from Pienza, is Sangallo's masterpiece, the Madonna di San Biagio, built in the form of a Greek cross, with a dome and two towers (one unfinished) flanking the façade, but detached from it. The building, which closely resembles Bramante's design for St Peter's, is one of the most beautiful and dignified churches I have seen, and I am not at all surprised that Sangallo built himself a charming house with a loggia of two storeys within 100 metres of it. The one building is worthy of the other.

Chiusi – the Clusium of Lars Porsenna and one of the 12 cities of the Etruscan Federation – I found disappointing. It stands high – 400 metres – and has splendid views over the Chiana valley, but the fact that it had been so important in Etruscan times had led me to expect that it would have retained its importance in subsequent centuries. This it failed to do. The Duomo dates from the twelfth century, but it has been restored to excess and few of the Roman or Etruscan inscriptions on the walls of the loggia in the square in front of it are clear enough to arouse one's interest. Apparently, at one time, the Chief Magistrate of Chiusi used to go out once a year on the Lake of Chiusi to marry it, as the Doges of Venice went out to be wedded to the sea, but even that picturesque but archaic ceremony no longer takes place.

But for Etruscologists, Chiusi, of course, still has great attractions. On the Piazza del Duomo stands a handsome twelfth-century tower beneath which one can visit a large Etruscan or Roman cistern, and one is assured that below the surface of the soil there are endless passages, which may be only sewers, but which have been closed up for fear of accidents or because they were filled with water. If they were sewers, they were sewers on a very considerable scale – Dennis writes of two 'underground streets, about three feet wide and ten high, partly built up with large square blocks of travertine', and he reports that in 1830 workmen busy in the Piazza del Duomo found four round holes, two feet in diameter, which gave lighting to a large square chamber, vaulted over with great blocks of travertine. Pliny claimed that King Porsenna 'rests under the town of Clusium', and described a monument of such fantastic size that it could scarcely have escaped the researches of modern archaeologists. If I were given permission to potter about somewhere as an amateur excavator, I think I would choose the country around Chiusi – when I sat down on some stone, exhausted and discouraged by my failure to dig up a few exquisite bronzes, I should at least have the consolation of a view before me as peaceful and beautiful as any in Central Italy.

Modern Etruscologists tend to emphasise the differences between the Etruscan cities rather than their points of similarity. Chiusi museum has its rectangular urns similar to those of Volterra, but it has also round ones, known as 'canopic' urns, made generally of bronze or pottery and capped by the reproduction of a human head, presumably the likeness of the individual whose ashes the urn contained. These canopic urns became more and more complex, with the handles in the shape of arms, and finally developed into representations of the upper halves of human bodies. Most of the urns at Chiusi were made of a soft local stone, called *pietra fetida* because it gives off an unpleasant smell when scratched or scraped. Chiusi used also to specialise in the production of that black 'Bucchero' pottery, of which copies are so often sold to tourists as the genuine article. (The illegal export of Etruscan antiquities, mainly from tombs that are broken into at night, is valued at about one million pounds a year, and the sale of forgeries is also not to be despised – I read somewhere that bronzes can be 'aged' rapidly and successfully with the use of a mixture of salt, saltpetre, horse-dung and urine.)

One of the most interesting of all Tuscan tombs, excluding those of Tarquinia, is the so-called Tomb of the Monkey, five kilometres north of Chiusi, dating back to the fifth century B.C. The entrance leads into a large room, with three other rooms opening out of it. It contains several pictures, most of which deal with sports or games. The monkey that gives the tomb its name is a small animal tied to a tree and watching two men wrestling. Another tomb, the Tomb of the Two Chariots, is interesting in that its wall paintings include a false door, designed to make the tomb look larger and more important than it is – an early example of *'trompe l'oeil'* which became so popular in Italy during and after the Renaissance.

In this book I have, as far as possible, kept away from *autostrade*, not because I underestimate the importance and often – as between Bologna and Florence – the beauty of these speedways, but because, in order to get you quickly from one place to another, they must avoid all towns. My object, of course, is precisely the opposite – to interest you in a good many towns the man in a hurry would miss. But, at least from Chiusi to Orvieto I would advise the use of the *Autostrada del Sole* – the time gained can be employed so pleasantly in the latter town.

Orvieto's appearance is well known, up there on its great and precipitous *tufa* rock – rock deriving from the tightly-packed volcanic ash, so porous and absorbent that I am told its houses, high above the plain, are unusually cold and damp in the rainy season. The first view for anybody arriving by road from the north or by *autostrada* or train from either direction is not attractive, for there is an ugly conglomeration of factories, workshops, garages and box-like blocks of flats at the foot of the hill. The really dramatic view, and one which nobody with a car should miss, is from the road from Rome by way of Viterbo and Montefiascone. Ten minutes will take you there, ten minutes will bring you back, and the time you spend by the roadside staring at the town on its immense rock will depend upon your appreciation of an extraordinary view.

One's first visit in Orvieto is likely to be to the Duomo, which is so obviously the most important building in the town. Baedeker refers to it as 'a magnificent example of the Italian Gothic style, and one of the most interesting edifices in Italy'. The Italian Touring Club guide says 'it is one of the most significant creations of Italian Gothic architecture'. The Michelin *Guide Vert* calls it 'a perfect example of transitional Romanesque-Gothic style'. It was begun in 1295, and its bronze doors, by a contemporary artist named Emilio Greco, were hung only in 1970 – after several years of bitter controversy between those who admire them (as I do) and those who argue that they are out of keeping with the rest of the building. But since 33 architects, 152 sculptors, 68 painters, and 90 workers in mosaics are said to have made their contributions to the building, it is difficult to decide what part of it should be in keeping with what other part of it.

Despite the laudatory quotations with which I began the last paragraph, I still cannot pretend to like the Duomo. As I have already written in the chapter on Siena, I find the vertical pillars entirely lacking in the spiritual aspiration of French and English Gothic, despite the little needle-like spires at the top of them. Orcagna's very elegant rose window is spoilt for me by its square framework containing 52 heads of prophets and apostles. The mosaics above the doors and in the three pointed gables, dealing with the life of the Virgin, make me remember with nostalgia the superb mosaics of Ravenna. The pointed arch gave the opportunity for exciting developments in architecture but, placed above the three rounded arches in Orvieto, I find them unnecessary to the extent of being ugly. But then I am not an expert in architecture – I know only that, at any rate in Italy, I prefer Romanesque arches to Gothic isosceles triangles, and I dislike the mixture of both of them.

Obviously, there must be a lot that pleases in a building to which so many great artists contributed, and the bas-reliefs on the four pilasters seem to me very beautiful. Those to the left of the main entrance (from left to right and from bottom to top) deal with stories from the Old Testament; those to the right deal with the New Testament. Apparently, at one time they were coloured, but fortunately they have now weathered to the colour of old ivory. Their details are still so clear and sharp that it is difficult to believe they were carved by the Sienese artist, Lorenzo Maitani, before 1330.

The flamboyance of the façade at least has the merit of increasing one's appreciation of the sober interior. Two chapels attract most attention – the *Cappella del Corporale* in the north transept and the *Cappella della Madonna di San Brizio* in the southern one. The former contains the relic which caused the whole cathedral to be built and which gave rise to the annual festival (on 25 May) of *Corpus Domini*. In 1263, a young Bohemian priest on a pilgrimage to Rome had doubts about the doctrine of transubstantiation while he was saying mass in a chapel at Bolsena, but when he broke the Eucharistic wafer blood began to drip from it on to the chalice cloth (*corporale*). This *corporale* was brought to Pope Urban iv, who was in Orvieto, and he decided that so important a relic at a time when there were so many sceptics and heretics deserved a splendid church to house it and a special day for its commemoration. The silver reliquary in which this much-revered relic is kept is a magnificent example of fourteenth-century goldsmith's art, enriched with enamels and precious stones. It weighs upwards of 100 kilogrammes and is a metre and a half in height. Except by special favour, the *corporale* is on display only on Easter Sunday and on 25 May.

In the *Madonna di San Brizio* chapel only two of the panels of the vaulting – Christ in Judgment and the Assembly of Prophets – are by Fra Angelico, whose work had already won great praise in Rome. But he was called away, and 52 years elapsed before, in 1499, Luca Signorelli from Cortona, was commissioned to complete Fra Angelico's unfinished work. For the next four years, Signorelli was busy painting his frescoes of the apocalypse, the vigour of which reminds one of Michelangelo's ceiling in the Sistine Chapel. The plastic qualities of Signorelli's work, achieved only three or four years earlier by the liberal use of white paint in his frescoes at Monte Oliveto Maggiore, are still more remarkable here, although achieved by much subtler methods. The Resurrection of the Body, with skeletons struggling out of their tombs and recovering flesh, muscles and joy of life must surely place him in the very first rank, if not of painters, at least of innovators with paint. The two figures in the bottom left-hand corner of his 'Overthrow of Anti-Christ' are said to be portraits of himself and Fra Angelico.

The first pope to live in the Palazzo dei Papi (now the Museum) was Hadrian iv, the only English pope. He was also the first to recognise Orvieto's communal administration in

1157, but this transfer of some power to the people did not save Orvieto from generations of even bloodier feuds between ruling families than were experienced in most other Italian cities. And yet work on the Duomo went on – for example while Andrea Pisano was finishing the statue of the Madonna and Child which now stands above the main doorway, one Ghibelline leader from Orvieto was being dragged through the streets of Rome in a cage on wheels, while his captors grabbed bits of his flesh with red-hot pincers.

Several other popes found refuge in Orvieto, whose leading citizens were Guelfs, and therefore favourable to the papacy in its troubles with the emperors, and whose position made it so nearly impregnable. It would be a pity to leave Orvieto without doing two things – drinking some of its excellent dry white wine and visiting the Pozzo di San Patrizio, made on the orders of Pope Clement VII by Antonio Sangallo, nephew of Antonio Sangallo il Vecchio, who did so much to beautify Montepulciano.

Clement VII, nephew of Lorenzo de' Medici, was Pope in 1527, during the Sack of Rome by an appalling rabble of Germans, Italians and Spaniards under the command of the renegade Constable of Bourbon – 'Constable' being the name by which the commander of the French forces was known at that time. The pope escaped from St Peter's to the neighbouring Castel Sant'Angelo along a corridor that had been built on the orders of one of his predecessors, the Borgia Pope, Alexander VI. After being besieged there for a month, Clement surrendered and promised to pay a very large ransom. While awaiting its collection, he escaped to Orvieto where, fearing a breakdown in the water supply in the event of another siege, he organised the sinking of a remarkable well, later called the Pozzo di San Patrizio.

This is an extraordinary affair – a well 63 metres deep and 13 metres in diameter, with two separate spiral staircases winding round the outside of its shaft, so that men or donkeys could go down to fetch water by one staircase and come up by another.

The quickest way from Orvieto to Rome is, of course, along the *autostrada* but to take it would be a grave error of judgment, for one would then bypass not only Viterbo, which is certainly one of the most interesting cities in Italy, but also the little town of Montefiascone. A very slight detour to Bolsena also enables one to drive the length of the lake of that name. This lake may or may not be in the crater of an extinct volcano, as is the near-by, and even more beautiful, Lake of Bracciano, but the whole of this region is volcanic in origin and the lake has the very considerable maximum depth of 146 metres (as against only seven metres in the even larger lake of Trasimeno, near Perugia). Its eels were mentioned by Dante, and it is alleged that the surfeit of eels that caused the death of Pope Martin IV in the thirteenth century was brought to Perugia from this lake.

At the southern end of the lake is Montefiascone, attractive in itself but famous for the '*est, est, est*' legend, which still, after many centuries, helps to sell the very good local wine. A German bishop, member of the famous Fugger family of merchant bankers from Augsburg, was in the habit of sending his valet ahead of him to find the best wine in the next place where he proposed to stay. On the door of each inn of his choice, the valet wrote '*est*' to denote that '*Vinum est bonum*' (the wine is good). He found it so good at Montefiascone that he wrote '*est, est, est*' and the prelate so fully agreed with this verdict that he remained in Montefiascone to drink himself to death. In the quaint church of San Flaviano – two churches built, the one above the other – there is a tombstone the time-worn inscription of which, in so far as it is still intelligible, seems to confirm the legend and to have been erected by the valet in memory of his master who died of 'too much *est, est, est*'.

*   *   *

Viterbo has particular associations for Catholics, since more popes stayed there than in any other city outside Rome – not even excluding Avignon, to which the headquarters of the Church were moved from 1309 to 1377. Viterbo is generally held to be the town in which took place the very dramatic first meeting between the Hohenstaufen leader, Frederick Barbarossa, on his way to Rome to be crowned Emperor of the Holy Roman Empire, and Hadrian IV, the English pope (Nicholas Breakspear), who was to crown him. Each wanted to assert his power. They met in 1155 near the picturesque mediaeval fountain in the Piazza della Morte and Hadrian insisted that the new Emperor should hold his stirrup while he dismounted – an act of submission which Frederick made, with great reluctance, because otherwise he might not have been crowned. (It is only fair to add that the two small neighbouring towns of Nepi and Sutri each claims to have been the place where this notable event in the long, long rivalry between popes and emperors took place. They are two small walled towns of Etruscan origin. Nepi's castle was built for the Borgia pope, Alexander VI, and Lucrezia Borgia lived there in 1500 after the death of her first husband. Sutri – like other Etruscan towns, built on the narrow crest of a steep hill – has a Roman amphitheatre dug out of the tufa rock.)

Barely 200 metres from Viterbo's Piazza della Morte is the Piazza del Duomo with the Cathedral and the Palace of the Popes, built on the site of the ancient acropolis. With its outside staircase and its beautiful loggia, this is an example of Italian Gothic at its most impressive best. The loggia has all the elegance of one of the great French cathedrals, with the clearness of an Italian sky behind it. This palace is also, of course, a building of great historic importance – it was here that, after the death of a French pope in 1268, a conclave of cardinals met for two years without being able to agree on his successor, although the local magistrates ended up by locking them in the great hall with little food and water and by removing the roof which, in the words of one cardinal, prevented the Holy Spirit from descending to them. The first act of Gregory X, the pope who was finally elected, was to lay down rules for future conclaves for papal elections which are substantially those still in use. (The very word, conclave, is a reminder of the Viterbo muddle, *clavis* being the Latin word for a key.)

Fortunately for the visitor, Viterbo is a small town and its many treasures are more concentrated than in most towns. The Duomo and the Palazzo Papale are quite close to the walls, and to reach the central square, the Piazza del Plebiscito, the normal road to follow is the picturesque Via San Lorenzo. This will take you past the Chiesa del Gesù, which is generally held to be the church in which, in 1271, Guy de Montfort murdered Henry, the son of Richard, earl of Cornwall and nephew of Henry III, to avenge the death of his father at the battle of Evesham (for which crime Dante, in his *Inferno*, condemned Guy to the Seventh Region of Hell).

But the shortest way is not always the best way, and one should on no account miss the San Pellegrino quarter, as mediaeval in appearance as the old quarter of Perugia. In the tiny Piazza San Pellegrino there is a charming but dilapidated Palazzo Alessandri, whose owners were very prominent supporters of the Gatti family in the fights against supporters of the rival Tignosi family – *plus les noms changent, plus c'est la même chose*! Generation after generation of the Alessandri are said to have kept a cauldron of oil always on the boil, ready in case of attack. How, one wonders, did people who were so bloody-minded build cities that are so outstandingly beautiful? One of the particularly beautiful features of Viterbo is the number of its elegant fountains. Walking from the Piazza San Pellegrino, you can pass the most original of them, the fourteenth-century Fontana Grande, on your way to the Piazza del Plebiscito, the centre of the town, where there is another very graceful seventeenth-century fountain in the courtyard of the Palazzo Comunale. Viterbo has been called 'the city of fine fountains and beautiful women'.

Outside the church of St Angelo, between the Palazzo Comunale and the Palazzo del Podestà, there is a Roman sarcophagus which is supposed to contain the bones of Galiana, whose beauty led to a war in the twelfth century between ruling families in Viterbo and Rome. She was so fair, it was said, that when she drank red wine it could be seen as it passed down her throat.

The patron saint of Viterbo is Santa Rosa, who died in 1252 at the early age of 17. Every year on September 3, her gentleness and good work for the poor are, rather strangely, commemorated by 80 strong men who carry through the town a wooden trophy some 20 metres in height and weighing some 3,000 kilogrammes. By historians, Santa Rosa is remembered less for her saintliness than for the rather unsaintly vehemence of her campaign of hatred against the Emperor Frederick II ('*Stupor Mundi*'), who unsuccessfully besieged the town in 1243.

7. Florence, City of the Lily

What can a book that is not a guidebook say about such a city as Florence? Books about that city exist by the dozen, and dozens of other cities must be mentioned in this one short book. What are the qualities that have made it beloved above almost all cities? Its climate is unattractive – lying in a deep hollow, it can be appallingly hot in summer, and the winds off the snow-capped Apennines can make it appallingly cold in winter. On the other hand, the foothills come so close to the centre of the city that, from Piazzale Michelangelo, from Fiesole, from Bellosguardo or from the Boboli Gardens, one has fantastic views of its mediaeval roofs and towers. One expects the Arno to be romantic, as one expects the Danube to be blue, and in both cases one is disappointed. For most of the year, Italy's famous river is an insignificant yellow stream, meandering between banks of sand and shockingly tainted with rubbish – the only time in my experience when it showed the speed and strength one associates with a great river was during the floods of November, 1966; nobody who saw it then could ever again treat it with contempt. But what beauty is given it by its bridges and the *palazzi* along its banks! Is there another bridge anywhere as famous as the Ponte Vecchio? Even Hitler decided it must be spared, although the Germans destroyed every other bridge across the Arno, including the most beautiful of them, the Ponte Santa Trinità, which the German consul tried so hard to save that he became known as the Consul for

Florence. (Fortunately, it has been rebuilt – a perfect copy of its predecessor.)

Nor is Florence very old as Italian cities go. Fiesole was a well-known Etruscan town before Florence existed, but the building of the Via Cassia and of a bridge across the river where the Ponte Vecchio now stands soon gave it importance – then, as now, it stood near the junction of great roads running north and south and east and west. It became a Roman colony in 59 B.C., the year after Caesar, Pompey and Crassus had met in Lucca to form their triumvirate, and the Piazza della Repubblica, where one sits outside some café to rest one's weary feet, is built where the forum once stood. By 1125, after Florence had defeated Fiesole in a war that lasted for more than two years, Florence had become powerful enough to organise a league of Tuscan towns to resist the various invading armies from north of the Alps (including those of the Holy Roman Emperor himself). The league did not last long; the rivalries between these towns were too strong. But, as I suggested in the opening chapter, with the popes established in Avignon and the emperors also keeping out of Italy for most of their time, the Italian city states learnt to stand on their own and, despite the tragic absurdity of the Guelf–Ghibelline civil wars, some of them prospered.

None more so than Florence, which derived great wealth not only from its exports of wool and silks but also from the *expertise* of its bankers. Venice, Florence and Milan had become the great banking centres of Italy. (Bankers from Lombardy opened up in London's Lombard Street in the thirteenth century.) In the period of the early Renaissance, the fifteenth century, Venice was having trouble with her trade in the Eastern Mediterranean (especially after the Turks had captured Constantinople in 1453) and this worked to the advantage of the great banking families in Florence. They became as influential as some of the kings who depended upon them for money – it is said that Edward III of England won the Battle of Crécy as much because he had borrowed so considerably

18 *Ravenna: the mausoleum of Galla Placidia*

from Florentine bankers as because his longbowmen were so effective. The florin, of course, derives its name from a gold coin called the *fiorino*, which had the Florentine lily stamped on one side of it.

The Medici were not the first of the great Florentine banking families – they had been preceded by others whose names are commemorated in the Lungarno Acciaioli, Via dei Bardi, Piazza dei Peruzzi, Piazza dei Frescobaldi and others. The growing prosperity of the city was barely checked by the bankruptcy of the Bardi and the Peruzzi, as sensational in their age as the collapse of the Austrian Kredit-Anstalt was in the winter of 1929, but with much less disastrous results. Another banker who ended as a bankrupt was Luca Pitti, an enemy of Cosimo the Elder. He built the enormous Pitti palace (later inhabited by descendants of Cosimo) to house his family which, 'thanks to God is abundant', in the luxury to which they were accustomed. But, after he had gone bankrupt, 'even his old friends and relatives', according to Macchiavelli, 'were afraid to be seen walking down the street with him'. The banking centre of Florence was the so-called *Mercato Nuovo*, where foreigners now go to buy their straw and leather presents and to stroke the snout of the bronze boar (a copy; the original is in the Uffizi), which is a great favourite among the Florentines. There the bankers sat, behind their green baize tables.

Cosimo de' Medici – Cosimo the Elder, as he later was called, to distinguish him from the Grand Duke Cosimo I (1519-74) – lived from 1389 to 1464. He came of sturdy and shrewd farming stock, was generous with his money, especially in his encouragement of the arts, and built up his political power by professing to have no interest in politics. His *palazzo* – Palazzo Medici Riccardi, in the Via Cavour – was one of the first great buildings of the Renaissance, and one of the three (the others being the Palazzo Pitti and the Palazzo Strozzi) to be built in what is called *rustica* style, which is distinguished by its immense blocks of undressed stone and which has obviously been copied from the Etruscans. This 'rustication' and the emphasis on horizontal lines may at first offend Northern Europeans, more accustomed to the vertical exuberance of so much Gothic; it may seem almost brutally heavy. But by degrees they – or most of them – come to appreciate the studied simplicity that so marked the work of the early Renaissance architects. The differing treatment given to each storey, the careful proportion of the windows and doorways, and the widely projecting cornices give a sense of completeness that is often lacking in the contrived exaltation of Gothic buildings.

Cosimo the Elder gave many artists their opportunity – Donatello, whose work can best be seen in the Bargello Museum; Michelozzo, who built the Palazzo Medici Riccardi; Brunelleschi, whose dome over the Cathedral was rightly looked upon as one of the engineering marvels of the world; Fra Filippo Lippi, who chose such beautiful models for his Madonnas. But it was his grandson, Lorenzo, who earned the title of '*il Magnifico*'. He died in 1492, at the age of only 43, and with his death the greatest days of his family and of Florence were over. He was ugly, ruthless (as one had to be), but charming, intelligent and a brilliant statesman. I wonder whether any man has ever done more to advance a nation's culture. His huge *palazzo* gave shelter to many of the greatest artists including Michelangelo, and meetings were held here of the Platonic Academy, which had been founded by his grandfather, whose interest in Greek philosophy was as great as was the interest of Renaissance artists in Greek sculpture and architecture. (The *palazzo* was also the home of two future popes. One was Lorenzo's own son, Giovanni, who became Pope Leo X, after being made a cardinal at the age of fourteen. Cardinals, in those days, had not necessarily been ordained priests.) His promotion to the papal throne was even more precipitate – he was ordained to the priesthood on 13 March, 1513, consecrated bishop on the 17th, and enthroned on the 19th.) It was Leo X who made Wolsey a cardinal, and it was he whose unorthodox ways of raising funds shocked Martin Luther into revolt. The other future pope for whom the Palazzo Medici was home was Lorenzo's nephew, Giulio, who became Clement vii, pope when the army of the Emperor Charles v sacked Rome in 1527. He escaped from the Vatican along the corridor that leads to the Castel Sant' Angelo, where one man besieged with him was the splendid Florentine artist (and liar), Benvenuto Cellini. Cellini's grim but incomparable 'Perseus with the head of Medusa' is the finest piece of sculpture in Florence's *Loggia dei Lanzi*.

Unlike his grandfather, Lorenzo made few attempts to conceal his love of power. In his dealings with foreign states, he was generally wise and astute, but he was ruthless in dealing with potential rivals inside Florence. Despite the heavy taxes needed to maintain so luxurious a court, he retained his popularity with the masses by a pageantry that resembled the 'bread and circuses' policy of the Roman emperors, but that was inspired by far more affection. He was a moderately good poet, and enjoyed singing his ballads in the streets although – or, more probably, because – many of them were, in the words of the *Encyclopaedia Britannica*, 'often of a most revolting nature'. Above all, of course, he encouraged artists, writers, philosophers, historians – everybody, in fact, who had intelligence and an enquiring mind.

As far as Lorenzo's ruthless destruction of his rivals is concerned, his treatment of the Pazzi conspiracy is a remarkable instance of the cruelty and crime that existed even in this most civilised of cities. Visitors to Florence should on no account miss the great Franciscan church of Santa Croce, which stands in one of the poorer quarters, behind the Uffizi and the Palazzo della Signoria. It is a low-lying quarter, and s̄ ̄ered very badly from the floods of 1966 – I went through street after street in which the water had risen above the windows of the first floor; rushing into the cellars, it had burst through the floors on ground level; it caused very considerable damage inside Santa Croce itself. Fortunately, it did not greatly damage the Giotto frescoes or the tombs of some of Italy's greatest men – Michelangelo, Machiavelli, Galileo,

Ugo Foscolo and the poet Alfieri, with whom the wife of
Bonnie Prince Charlie lived (in a *palazzo* which now houses
the British consulate) when the Stuart prince's dissipation and
jealousy had driven her to leave him.

Nor did the floods greatly damage the Pazzi chapel, which
one enters through a cloister at the side of Santa Croce and
which Brunelleschi built between 1430 and 1446 – possibly
an even greater masterpiece than the dome of the Cathedral.
The Pazzi were a very aristocratic family, whose members
probably thought of Cosimo and other early Medici as parve-
nus. Like the Medici, they were bankers, and Francesco Pazzi,
established in Rome, saw his opportunity to destroy Medici
rule in Florence when Lorenzo refused to lend Pope Sixtus IV
a large sum of money. This he refused to do because the money
would have enabled the pope's singularly evil nephew, Girolamo Riario, to establish himself at Imola, too close to Florence for Lorenzo's comfort.

Sixtus (to whom posterity owes gratitude, since he inaugur-
ated the building of the Sistine Chapel in Rome) was furious.
Besides transferring his overdraft from the Medici to the Pazzi,
he encouraged Francesco to remove Lorenzo from power. He
explained that he did not want any killings but he was perfectly well aware of the nature of the thugs who joined in
the conspiracy. Only one of them was, on the face of it,
respectable – Archbishop Salviati of Pisa.

The opportunity for action came after the Pope had nom-
inated a 20-year-old nephew to be a cardinal. This young man
was to pass through Florence, and he invited Lorenzo and his
brother, Giuliano, to dine. But Giuliano was unwell, and the
conspirators wanted to remove rivalry by killing both the
Medici. A few days later, the Medici invited the young cardinal
to dine at the Medici villa in Fiesole, but again Giuliano was
absent and the jovial occasion did not end in murder. Time
was getting short, and it was decided that both brothers should
be killed on Sunday during high mass in the cathedral – an
occasion when men are most easily caught off their guard. The

soldier of fortune who had been selected to stab Lorenzo was the only member of the group who was so shocked by this plan to commit murder in church that he refused to co-operate (which did not save him from execution when the whole affair was over), and two young priests agreed to replace him. They bungled; Giuliano was stabbed to death but Lorenzo, slightly wounded in the neck, managed to reach the sacristy and to lock himself in.

Meanwhile, Archbishop Salviati and others had gone to the Palazzo della Signoria, expecting to take over the government. But the crowd had heard of the events in the Duomo. Francesco Pazzi, Salviati and others were hanged by their feet from the windows of the Signoria. Less important conspirators were killed, cut up by the angry crowds, and the pieces were carried on sticks in triumph round the city. Jacopo Pazzi, the head of the family, was buried in Santa Croce, but the rumour went around that he had sold his soul to Satan, so he was reburied in ground that was not holy. Even that would not suffice – his body was dug up again and dragged through the streets with little bells attached to the rotting corpse. The authorities had his body thrown into the Arno, but downstream some children dragged it out again, hanged it from a tree and amused themselves by beating it. Finally, it was thrown back into the river. Altogether some 270 people were killed. One of the assassins who stabbed Giuliano escaped and took refuge in Constantinople, but Lorenzo demanded his extradition; he was brought back to Florence and hanged. The remaining members of the Pazzi family were shut up in a dungeon in Volterra. The name and the coat of arms of the Pazzi family were removed from every document and every public place.

Probably because the Medici were men of so many interests, one of the remarkable features about the artists of the Renaissance was the variety of their activities. I have mentioned Brunelleschi's dome of the Cathedral and his Pazzi chapel. He was also a goldsmith. So was Ghiberti, who made two of the three bronze doors of the Baptistery. Benvenuto Cellini made the Perseus in the Loggia dei Lanzi, but he also did exquisite silver work (and he wrote one of the most entertaining auto-biographies in existence). The Pollaiuolo brothers were painters, sculptors, engravers, goldsmiths and designers of embroidery. Michelangelo was famous not only as a sculptor but also as an architect. And Leonardo da Vinci was the Universal Man. He was a great painter, and yet seems often to have been less interested in painting than in anatomy and mechanics. He invented the first armoured car, anticipated the helicopter and the submarine, and made the first aeroplane, which is said to have been launched from the hill just east of Fiesole. The machine crashed, but he was nevertheless some four centuries ahead of others in the science of aeronautics. Other children of his brain were an instrument for measuring wind speeds, a parachute and a kind of life-belt, and during his years in Milan he spent much of his time draining marshes and building fortifications.

Another factor besides the generous patronage of the Medici and other families helped the artists in Florence. Partly to check the influence of an idle aristocracy, and to bring them more or less to the level of other people, it was decreed that everybody must belong to one of the guilds if he wanted to enjoy civic rights. Painters and sculptors were in the same guild as doctors and apothecaries. They did not live away from ordinary people in ivory towers or, more probably, draughty attics. They were members of the community, and the community was proud of their achievements and their fame.

You see the outcome of this general interest in art if you cross the Ponte Vecchio or the Ponte Santa Trinità to what used to be called the 'new' quarter, although much of it dates back to the Middle Ages. For here, in crowded, dark workshops, you can watch carpenters and other craftsmen still working in conditions that must be very similar to those of the Renaissance. Many of them are restoring furniture that is 300 or 400 years old, and the final article may contain very little of the original wood. But their work is done with so much skill and appreciation of artistic beauty that I, for one, make no complaint if something they sell me contains nothing genuinely old except the wood, taken from some other piece that had decayed beyond repair. These craftsmen, working in cellars or on the ground floor, suffered very severely from the 1966 floods; had they been put out of business, the world would have been much the poorer for it.

And therein lies one of the secrets of Florence's attraction – people, however modest their education, must inevitably be influenced by the beauty round them. Except in the new suburbs, as hideous in Florence as elsewhere in Italy, almost every street contains buildings the good proportions of which have since been copied in almost every other country. Almost every church contains one or more paintings by artists whose other works are proudly displayed in art galleries around the world. Familiarity with Michelangelo's 'David' in the Piazza della Signoria (only a copy, but a very good one) or Cellini's 'Perseus' or Giovanni da Bologna's 'Rape of the Sabines' (both in the Loggia dei Lanzi) does not breed contempt, even if you pass them every day on your way to work. In Florence, even more than in Rome, one is constantly aware of being in a civilised city.

Foreigners tend to congregate in two places – round the Duomo or on the Piazza della Signoria and its neighbouring Ponte Vecchio. Both are so well-known that I add only a very few details to the information contained in even the smallest guide or folder. The façade of the Duomo is modern – it dates from the second half of the nineteenth century – but the building itself was started in 1296 by Arnolfo di Cambio, and excavations in progress under the nave have already revealed very interesting remains of the much older church of Santa Reparata which had been used as the cathedral from 1128 onwards. Arnolfo di Cambio died in 1402, and nothing was done for another thirty years. Brunelleschi completed the dome only in 1434, and the lantern on the top of it, also designed by him, was added in 1461, 15 years after his death.

Few buildings have given rise to so much controversy. 1417 arrived before any one of the successive architects raised a stone of the cupola. Brunelleschi was so vague and confusing about details that on one occasion he was treated as a madman and thrown out of the meeting of prominent citizens who had met to examine his plans. Lorenzo Ghiberti, who made two of the bronze doors of the Baptistery, was brought in to help him, whereupon he went to bed and stayed there until Ghiberti was removed. Various experts were invited to give their opinions as to how the cupola could be erected, and their suggestions were not of a nature to arouse confidence. One suggestion was that it should be made of pumice stone, for the sake of its lightness. Another was that the building should be filled with a mountain of earth containing a lot of coins of low value. When the dome had been built over this mountain, the Florentines would willingly carry it all away again in order to get at the coins. Yet another idea was that the dome should be supported by a huge pole in the centre, like the pole that supports a tent. Such absurd propositions, put forward by serious Tuscan and foreign artists, underline the revolutionary nature of Brunelleschi's own plans.

The base of the cupola has an unfinished look, and Brunelleschi had planned to make a gallery round it, but this plan was mislaid. Sixty years after his death, another architect began to make this gallery, but Michelangelo − in, I imagine, one of his more bitter and jealous moods − said that it reminded him of the little cages in which Florentine children put grasshoppers, and the plan was dropped. Part of this gallery, which I venture to find quite elegant and preferable to a good many of the Duomo's floridly decorative features, can still be seen at the south-eastern corner of the building. Near this south-eastern corner is a stone (now let into a wall) which is called the *Sasso di Dante* (Dante's stone) because it was here that he used to sit in the cool of the evening.

Giotto began to build the campanile in 1348. His instructions were to make it 'so magnificent that, by its height and the quality of the work put into it, it shall exceed everything of the kind ever made by the Greeks or the Romans at the summit of their power'. The tower is 84 metres high, and the foundations were dug to a depth of 16 – a hole which must have amazed the onlookers of those days. Giotto lived to supervise only a very little of the building, but he completed the first course of its sculptured ornamentation, and his general design was faithfully carried out. The 414 steps to the summit are said by Baedeker to be 'easy', and who am I to argue with Baedeker?

Inside the cathedral on the north wall there are large frescoes of two warriors on horseback. The one nearer the altar is of an Englishman, Sir John Hawkwood who, after fighting at Crécy, became one of the most famous of Italian condottieri, leading a mercenary army he called the White Company. He was known in Italy as Giovanni Acuto, his English name sounding too strange to the Italians. After fighting for years for the leader who paid him best, he became loyal to Florence and was appointed the city's commander-in-chief. He was promised that, after his death, the Florentines would erect an equestrian statue of him to equal those of other great condottieri, such as Gattamelata and Colleoni. Instead, the city fathers commissioned a fresco by Paolo Uccello, who was one of the early masters of that perspective known as *trompe l'oeil*, intended to deceive the eye into thinking that a fresco was, in fact, a fine marble statue.

The Baptistery is said to be the oldest building in Florence, and some experts claim that part of it dates back to the fifth century. Certainly it was considerably rebuilt at the very beginning of the thirteenth century at the expense of the wool merchant's guild, one of the most powerful in Florence. Originally, the centre of the dome was open to the sky. Its three bronze doors – that on the south side by Andrea Pisano, and those on the north and east by Ghiberti – are too well-known to call for comment from me. Brunelleschi, Donatello and Jacopo della Quercia were among Ghiberti's competitors for the commission. Michelangelo spoke for all subsequent generations when he said that the eastern door, the most recent of the three, made by Ghiberti between 1425 and 1452, was worthy to be the gates of Paradise. Apart from the famous mosaics that cover the immense space of the interior of the dome, one's attention is likely to be attracted by the beautiful tomb of Pope John XXIII. One reads that this is a masterpiece by Donatello who had his pupil, Michelozzo, to help him. But surely John XXIII was that lovable old man who died in 1964? How can this be?

The bones in the tomb are those of an 'anti-pope' – one of three men who claimed to have been legally elected to the papal throne after the death of Urban VI in the fourteenth century. For nearly forty years – the period known to historians as the Great Schism – some cardinals and countries had recognised a pope in Rome and others had recognised a pope in Avignon, and in 1409 an attempt was made at Pisa to end this schism by electing yet a third pope, who took the title of John XXIII. But the attempt failed; John was not accepted by the Council of Constance, and Martin V was elected in his place. Thus, since the Church had not recognised him as pope, the title became free for the John XXIII of this century.

The 'anti-pope', however, had been a friend of Cosimo de' Medici who commissioned Donatello to execute the tomb in the Baptistery. Martin V, who was living at Santa Maria Novella at the time, protested against the use of the words '*quondam Papa*' in the epitaph on the tomb, but the Florentines refused to erase them. Their Prior quoted the words of Pontius Pilate – 'What I have written, I have written'.

Foreigners are often puzzled by the magnificence of Italian baptisteries. The reason is that, in the Middle Ages, only bishops carried out the ceremony of Baptism, and they did so on only two or three occasions in the year. At other times, the baptistery would be kept closed, with the bishop's seal on the door. In the case of Florence, until the middle of the fifteenth century, baptisms took place only on Easter Saturday and on the Saturday before Pentecost. These were also occasions for taking a census of births – a black bean for a boy, a white one for a girl.

As in the case of many Italian churches in the Middle Ages, the baptistery was often used for civil functions – official welcomes to victorious troops, investitures of magistrates, coronations of poets and even political meetings.

You may notice two damaged porphyry columns outside the baptistery, flanking Ghiberti's famous Door to Paradise. They were presented to Florence by the Pisans to thank the Florentines for protecting their city while they were engaged in a campaign in the Balearic Islands in 1117. The columns are cracked, and the Florentines liked to claim that they had been cracked before they arrived, but that the damage had been hidden by a fine damask covering, whereas the Pisans, probably with truth, claimed that they were broken when floods in 1424 caused them to fall. In any case, they gave rise to a proverb about 'blind Florentines and treacherous Pisans'.

The Piazza della Signoria, even more than the Piazza del Duomo, is the hub of the foreign tourist's universe. And that includes the Ponte Vecchio, for one of the spokes includes a covered passage that stretches from the Uffizi gallery (the government offices in the days of the Renaissance), across the bridge, and then on to the Pitti Palace. This passage was built in 1564 by the artist, Vasari. The senior branch of the Medici family had died out in 1537, but the junior branch returned to power after eighteen years of exile and settled in the Palazzo Pitti. Recalling the escape of their ancestor, Pope Clement vii, along the overhead passage to the Castel St Angelo during the Sack of Rome, it seemed wise to the Medici in the Pitti Palace to have a way of escape in case of trouble. Hence the corridor along the rooftops of the goldsmiths on the upstream side of the Ponte Vecchio.

At least two bridges existed here before the present bridge. The first stone one was destroyed by the flood of November 1333 and nothing about the flood of 633 years later was more impressive than the way in which the water swept away the walls of the shops and yet left almost undamaged the structure of the bridge that had been built twelve years after the 1333 flood. For two centuries, the shops on the bridge had belonged to men of all trades, but mainly to butchers, who made the place even more disagreeable by leaving hides to soak in the river. It was Cosimo de' Medici, Grand Duke of Tuscany, who ordered in 1565 that these tradesmen should be replaced by goldsmiths. (His granddaughter, Marie de' Medici, married King Henry IV of France, and one of her daughters married King Charles I of England.)

The Piazza della Signoria has, of course, witnessed many extraordinary scenes. The most dramatic of them, I suppose, was the execution of Savonarola, a monk in the monastery of San Marco, whose fervent Christianity and reformist zeal so aroused the Florentines that they went around in the drabbest of clothes and spent Carnival in bringing their luxuries to be burned in great bonfires on the piazza. Unfortunately for posterity, several works of art, including studies by Lorenzo di Credi and Fra Bartolomeo, were destroyed as well as the wigs, perfumes, trinkets and books. The pope at the time was Alexander VI, a member of the notorious Borgia family, whose behaviour certainly justified Savonarola in his attacks against the papacy. One is shown the spot on the piazza where the monk met the violent end that he himself had made inevitable – with two of his closest supporters, he was hanged there and bundles of faggots were set alight beneath their bodies. The round stone let into the pavement to record this event – and to apologise for it – is a few yards in front of the Neptune fountain.

Three years later, the army of the Emperor Charles V had sacked Rome, and was sent to besiege Florence. Halfway through the ten months of siege, the Florentines played their traditional football match on the piazza in front of Santa Croce, and the event is now celebrated every year on the Piazza della Signoria in what is certainly the strangest and most picturesque football match in the world.

Florence had been divided into four quarters in the fourteenth century, and football matches between them had long been an annual event, played in different parts of the city. Santa

Croce provided the nearest open space to the imperial troops on the hill above and behind the present Piazzale Michelangelo, and it was there that the match was held on 17 February 1530 in order to impress the besiegers with the courage and fitness of the defenders. (In the words of the 1969 edition of a glossy and well-illustrated booklet, the aim of these football contests was to show 'the sumptuous courage and rabidness of the match', in which young people of noble families were encouraged to take part in order to show not only 'the stiliness and sumptuousness of the uniform but also their own strength and combativeness, rising always the admiration of the present gentle ladies'.)

There are 27 players in each team, and 'the play is to be considered a fusion of fights of rugby and football.... With every marking of a point the teams change the camp, while the score is ratified and notified to the public by means of elevation of signalling fans.... The two team captains have to appease quarrels and souls of their own players'.

I resist the temptation to describe very fully the colourful procession that precedes and concludes the game while 'the pealing of the Torre di Arnolfo tolls fiercely and joyously'. There are 'infantry officers in multi-coloured uniform cut and carved in many ways'. There are 'arquebusiers with sparkling morion in ship form'. There are 'Captains of the Bends' and 'Broken Barges, noblemen escort of the Major, General Sergeant'. And so on. But I suspect that the foreign onlooker would soon find somebody in the crowd who would explain matters more helpfully than the translators of this booklet.

No open place in the world contains so many works by famous sculptors as the Piazza della Signoria. They are too numerous and too well-known to be mentioned in detail. Not all of them are masterpieces – the Florentines themselves are very uncomplimentary about Ammanati's 'Neptune' – '*Il Biancone*' they call it, and this might, not unfairly, be translated as 'The great white lump'. And not all of them are genuine – the original of Michelangelo's 'David' is now in the Accademia di

Belli Arti, the original of Marzocco (the lion with a shield) is with many other works by Donatello in the Bargello museum; of the two lions that guard the steps up to the Loggia dei Lanzi, only the one farthest from the Palazzo Vecchio is antique – the other is 'modern' in that it dates from 1600.

Michelangelo was in his 20s when he sculpted his immense 'David', in the yard of the Opera del Duomo (the workshop for the restoration of or artistic improvements to the cathedral) and it took four days to move it to its place in front of the Palazzo Vecchio, in September 1504. Critics threw stones at it, and it had to have a military guard until it had been established on its terrace, where it came to be looked upon as a symbol of civic defiance of despots. The origin of the Marzocco is uncertain (although lions were associated with the idea of liberty). It is the heraldic emblem and the mascot of the city, and the name may come from 'Martiocus', meaning 'Little Mars'. It is as important to the Florentines as the Winged Lion is to the Venetians or the Wolf and Twins are to the Romans. In 1364, after the Florentines had defeated the Pisans, some two thousand prisoners were brought to Florence where they were compelled to kiss the Marzocco's backside – a reminder that the age of chivalry did not always result in chivalrous behaviour.

On the façade of the Palazzo Vecchio, near the corner of the Via della Ninna, you may notice the profile of a man's head incised on the wall. According to a not very credible legend, Michelangelo was talking to a friend one day and, with his hands behind his back, carved his friend's portrait during their conversation.

Every visitor must find his own Florence – the city has too many treasures even to be mentioned, let alone discussed. Santa Maria Novella, for example, has works by Ghirlandaio, Masaccio, Duccio di Buoninsegna, Filippino Lippi, Paolo Uccello, Brunelleschi, Orcagna and others. The tombs in Santa Croce include those of Dante (empty and unworthy), Michelangelo, Macchiavelli, Ghiberti and Rossini. The views of the city from the Piazzale Michelangelo or from Fiesole, and the villas along the roads to both these places, are unforgettable. I know of no other city with so many tablets to record the great men and women who have lived there. The list of famous visitors is endless – John Milton, Dostoievsky, Michael Faraday, Humphrey Davy, Goethe, Mikhail Bakunin, Mozart, Rainer Maria Rilke, the Brownings, Thomas Hobbes, Montaigne, Herman Melville, Mark Twain, Nietzsche, D. H. Lawrence, Handel, Liszt, Shelley, Ruskin, Walter Pater, Florence Nightingale, Lamartine, George Eliot – the attempt even to make a list of them is obviously absurd. There must be something quite extraordinary about Florence to have attracted people of so many nations and such varied achievements.

Maybe the attraction is its flowers. If I were called upon to put on canvas a scene most evocative of Florence, I should try to paint not the Ponte Vecchio or the Piazza della Signoria, but one of the narrow roads leading up to Bellosguardo or Fiesole, with high white walls surmounted by masses of mauve wistaria and with irises or roses at their base. A red lily (or, more accurately, an iris) on a white background is the emblem of Florence – the colours were reversed after 1251 when the Guelfs expelled the Ghibellines – and the most popular explanation of the city's name and coat of arms is that few other cities are so surrounded by flowers.

19   *Ravenna: the apse of Sant' Apollinare in Classe*

8. Arezzo and the Casentino

From which famous Italian city can you, in one day, visit the valleys of both Arno and Tiber; climb up to two of the country's most spectacular monasteries of which one was very closely associated with St Francis of Assisi; see the finest works of one of the most famous Italian painters, Piero della Francesca; potter about in a castle in which Dante spent part of his long exile; and, if you are not too weary, spend an hour or two in an excellent Etruscan museum? The answer is Arezzo.

Arezzo was an important city under both the Etruscans and the Romans – it was one of the 12 confederate cities of Etruria and it was the terminus of the Roman Via Cassia until after the Second Punic War (200 B.C.) when it lost much of its importance because the Via Cassia was extended through the upstart Florence and over the mountains to join the Via Emilia at Bologna. The Arezzo museum attracts numismatists on account of its fine collection of early coins, and it has a great many Roman vases of red terracotta, which originated here in Arezzo. It was the birthplace of many famous men. One of them was Vasari, the sixteenth-century painter and architect, whose works seldom win much praise, but whose biography of other artists has been an invaluable source-book for every writer about Renaissance art in Italy. The *Penguin Dictionary of Art and Artists* claims that it is 'perhaps the most important book on the history of art ever written'. The house that he built in Arezzo is now a museum.

Very much earlier in the town's history was Maecenas, whose encouragement to writers, and particularly to Virgil and Horace, has become proverbial. Guido d'Arezzo, a monk who invented the present system of musical notation, is supposed to have been born here at the end of the tenth century. Another citizen of Arezzo was Petrarch, generally considered to have been Italy's greatest lyric poet, although Byron did not share this view. He had little patience with Petrarch's over-delicate attitude towards his beloved Laura. 'Think you', he wrote, 'if Laura had been Petrarch's wife/He would have written sonnets all his life?'

A very different product was the sixteenth-century poet, pornographer, reformer, satirist, cad, rake, sycophant and black-mailer, Pietro Aretino, who got himself expelled from his home town when he was a very young man for writing a satirical and well-justified sonnet against the sale of religious indulgences. He was often called 'the divine Aretino' but it seems that the adjective was of his own attribution. He had periods when he enjoyed the favour of the pope, Francis I of France, and other great men of his time, but he offended them all. His last 30 years were spent in Venice where, according to legend, he died by falling off his chair when he was laughing at an indecent story told by his sister. I imagine that I should immensely have enjoyed his company in some tavern over a litre or two of wine, and have blamed him for my hangover next morning.

But it is for none of these distinguished citizens that one goes to Arezzo. The chief attraction is the church of San Francesco, where are Piero della Francesca's frescoes of the Legend of the True Cross – the chief attraction now; half a century ago this painter was not recognised as one of the very greatest artists of the Renaissance.

One should, however, take a look at the rest of Arezzo before visiting this church, which is likely to send you hurrying off to see Piero della Francesca's other masterpieces in the neighbourhood – 'The Resurrection' at Borgo San Sepolcro or the very beautiful 'Pregnant Madonna' in a little chapel at Monterchi.

The Piazza Grande, for example, should not be missed. It is on a fairly steep slope, which fact has given us a very unusual flight of steps. Near these steps is the apse of Santa Maria della Pieve, with its very elegant little loggia, and another feature of the square is the imposing Palazzo delle Loggie, built by Vasari. It is on this piazza that, on the first Sunday in June and September, there is a jousting tournament, when horsemen in fourteenth-century uniforms charge full tilt at a wooden figure, known as the 'Saracen' (a reminder of early invaders of Italy), and try with their lances to hit the bull's eye on the target that the figure holds. A bad shot causes the 'Saracen's' arm to swing round and to give the unsuccessful competitor a hefty whack on the back with a flail to which are attached three balls of lead.

The façade of Santa Maria della Pieve is even more remarkable than the apse, for it consists of five blind arches and three open colonnades, each of which is lower and narrower than the colonnade below it. As in so many other Pisan-Romanesque buildings, each column is differently shaped or carved and the resulting effect is both solid and elegant. Its tall, square tower is also unusual, in that it has four windows on each storey, whereas in most belfry towers of the period the number of windows decreases in the lower storeys. With pardonable exaggeration, it is generally known as the *'campanile delle cento buche'*, the 'tower of a hundred holes'. Vasari's house is worth a visit as a good example of the home of a prosperous artist of the Renaissance, and I find the Palazzo Pretoria attractive on account of the great number of coats of arms (with that of the Medici – large and prominent in the centre), which decorate its façade. They would have angered St Bernardino, who managed to get them banned from Siena because, as he rightly argued, this particular form of snobbishness was one of the main causes of the family feuds that caused so much misery in mediaeval Italy.

And now to San Francesco (with, if possible, some field-glasses, since several of Piero della Francesca's frescoes are high up on the walls and have suffered the ravages of time). They are also very confusing, since not many of us know the Golden Legend's Story of the True Cross and, being more mathematically than chronologically minded, Piero matched one event against another (e.g. Constantine's victory over Maxentius and the victory of Heraclius over the Persian king, Chosroes, who had used part of the Cross as a throne) so that events are not portrayed in chronological order. There is not much movement even in the battle scenes but the composition of each fresco is immensely impressive and the sense of colour is incomparable. One is not surprised that Lord Clark found the morning light in the battle picture of Constantine's victory the most perfect in all the painting of the Renaissance. Piero's clear, pale blue skies make me think of the sky above the Cornish coast on a day with a fresh summer breeze.

St Francis was, of course, much more closely associated with Assisi than with Arezzo, but from Arezzo, even more easily than from Florence, one can visit La Verna monastery, between the Casentino and the upper valley of the Tiber, where the saint received the stigmata – the first carefully documented case of an individual who miraculously develops wounds in his hands, his feet and his side similar to those suffered by Christ on the cross. The details as recorded in the *Little Flowers of St Francis* are too circumstantial to be rejected as legend. Having seen men in South East Asia walk across red-hot coals or suffer no pain or scar when skewers are thrust through their cheeks or tongue, I have long since ceased to express scepticism about things I do not understand, and I would rather believe miracles concerning St Francis than concerning any other follower of Christ.

When the saint, with three companions, set out to climb to the summit of La Verna, he was so weak that at one stage a peasant lent him his donkey to ride. The peasant urged him to 'try to be as good as thou art by all folk held to be ... and I therefore admonish thee that in thee there be naught save what men hope to find therein'. Whereupon St Francis, instead of being offended, 'threw himself from off the ass upon the ground, and kneeled down before him and kissed his feet, and then humbly thanked him for that he had deigned thus lovingly to admonish him. Then the peasant, together with the companions of St Francis, with great devotion, lifted him from the ground and set him on the ass again, and they went on their way ...'.

La Verna is less than 1,000 metres above sea-level and one can drive by car to the monastery gate. But the most suitable adjective I can find to describe it is 'awe-inspiring', for it is set on the summit of a cliff that falls almost vertically for some 250 metres and it is scored by deep clefts with over-hanging moss-covered rocks. Were it not for the circumambient atmosphere of gentleness and gaiety I always associate with Franciscans, I should find the place sinister and frightening. It is the sort of place which the Primitives liked as the background for their paintings of hermits resisting devils. With his favourite discipline, Brother Leo, St Francis found 'a horrible and fearful cleft in a huge rock', which could be crossed only on a tree trunk that acted as a kind of drawbridge, and they here made a little cell in which St Francis could be left to meditate. He was visited only once every day, when Brother Leo brought him bread and water, to be left on the other side of the cleft unless St Francis answered his call.

Here St Francis remained for 40 days. 'During all the time of that fast, a falcon that was building her nest hard by his cell awoke him every night a little before Matins with her singing and the beating of her wings against the cell.... And when perchance St Francis was too weary or weak, this falcon, like a discreet person and pitiful, would sing her song later ... and beyond all this she would sometimes in the daytime sit quite tamely by him.' When finally Francis left his sanctuary, his fellow-Franciscans found that 'his hands and his feet appeared to have been pierced through the middle with nails, and the heads of which were in the palms of his hands and the soles of his feet, outside the flesh ... and the heads of the nails were round and black. Likewise, in the right side appeared the image of a wound made by a lance, unhealed and red and bleeding'. Unable to walk, he had to be carried down the mountainside and, like Jesus entering Jerusalem, he rode back to Assisi on an ass. He died there two years later.

The nicest legend about St Francis is also associated with La Verna. After his death, a chapel was built at the place where he received the stigmata. On one occasion the weather was so bad that the brethren failed to visit it for midnight prayers. The next morning they were put to shame by the sight of bird and animal tracks in the snow leading to the chapel door. Stories of this sort, of course, endear him to the British, with their proverbial love of animals. But so do his humility and his gaiety. He seems to have lacked the deliberate intention to mortify the flesh which bewilders Englishmen who normally dislike extremes; if he starved himself, it was more because he was too engrossed in contemplation to worry about food than because he believed that it was good for his immortal soul to go hungry and unwashed.

His father had been a prosperous textile merchant in Assisi and, as a young man, Francis seems to have had few preoccupations beyond devising cheerful ways of spending his father's money. But at the age of 20 he was taken prisoner in a war between Arezzo and Perugia and spent a year in captivity. This, and a serious illness, entirely changed him; he began to devote all his time and a lot of his father's money to the poor and the sick, including the lepers of the nearby town of Gubbio, although he had a particular horror of leprosy. When his father summoned him before the bishop to disinherit him, he is said to have arrived naked, carrying his clothes and his cash, and saying that henceforward his only father was 'Him that is in Heaven'. He began to preach the virtues of poverty, chastity, humility, obedience, and led 12 of his disciples to Rome to ask the pope to bless their work among the poor.

The pope, Innocent III, must have hesitated to bless a movement that threatened to be revolutionary – there was so much corruption and luxury among the cardinals and high prelates that very few of them could have welcomed a campaign which inevitably would be directed against them. On the other hand, it was obvious that so sincere and gifted a young man could be of immense value to Christianity, and the pope gave him his blessing. Subsequent popes found it necessary to excommunicate some of the more ardent Franciscans, but even during the life of St Francis, friars wearing grey habits found their way as far afield as England. (Franciscans now wear brown; they formerly wore grey as that was the colour of the cheapest cloth obtainable, and it is in memory of St Francis that one finds a Greyfriars Street in some old English towns.) Well over 700 years after his death, people in many countries talk with reverence and affection of his cheerfulness, his humility and his charity. One need not be a Christian to be profoundly moved by a visit to La Verna.

The other famous monastery in the Casentino, the valley of the upper Arno, is the headquarters of a religious order of a very different kind, founded by a Benedictine monk half a century before the conquest of Britain by William the Conqueror. This Benedictine, who later became St Romuald, shared the indignation of St Francis over the lax morals of the Church (or, rather, antedated the Franciscan's indignation by a century and a half), and he established an Order of his own with its headquarters in the forest at Camaldoli. But, whereas the Franciscans hoped to reform the world by their own charity and goodness, the Camaldolese withdrew from the world and led the lives of hermits, in imitation of the earliest and strictest hermits of Egypt and Syria. At one time, there were many colonies, or 'deserts' as they were called, of Camaldolese hermits in central Italy and some in Germany, Poland and France. St Romuald had great influence over the Holy Roman Emperors of his time, Otto III and Henry II, and went on missions to heathen parts of eastern Europe – as a very old man, he died while on his way to Hungary. Lorenzo de' Medici's famous Platonic Academy sometimes met at Camaldoli. But by and large the hermits led, and still lead, a life of quite exceptional isolation.

How lonely, one begins to realise when one follows the steep road to the abbey. It stands at little more than 800 metres, but for much of the year it is under snow, and when I tried to visit it one April I found the road still blocked by trees that had fallen in the winter storms. Lay brothers run the farm and, two miles down the mountainside, an ancient pharmacy and a shop for holiday-makers, but the hermits themselves – now fewer than a score – have no contact with the outside world. They see each other seven times in the 24 hours in their church, but they do not speak. Twelve times a year they meet for a meal, eaten in silence, after which they may talk. As one of the lay brothers told H. V. Morton (*A Traveller in Italy*), they find little to say to each other on these occasions. 'One gets out of the habit'.

Behind and above the hermitage, from a place called the Prato al Soglio, one has a view that, on very clear days, is said to extend from the Adriatic in the east to the Tyrrhenian Sea near Pisa in the west. I take this piece of information from my Baedeker, for I have not myself climbed to the necessary height of nearly 1,500 metres. My own edition of Baedeker is dated 1912, and I am constantly amazed by the thoroughness with which its compilers explored the country in the days when most travel away from the railway line had to be by horse carriage. The introduction warns the foreigner that diarrhoea is very common in Italy and gives, as one of its causes, 'too strenuous travelling and sightseeing'. Of this, the compilers must have had plenty of experience.

What a fabulous region this is! St Francis received the stigmata at La Verna. Just down the hill to the south-east is San Sepolcro where Piero della Francesca was born, and where you can see his finest picture, 'The Resurrection', with Christ rising from the tomb around which four Roman soldiers lie awkwardly asleep. There is no other picture I would travel so far to see. A few miles away, also in the upper valley of the Tiber, is Caprese, the birthplace of Michelangelo. West of La Verna is the upper valley of the Arno, better known as the Casentino, and here Dante fought in a battle against the forces of Arezzo and later spent part of his exile. One might associate four such famous men with a large city, such as Rome or Florence, but not with this quiet and beautiful countryside, with only its ruined castles to remind one of its lurid past while they increase its present attractions.

In the disastrous wars between Guelfs and Ghibellines, Dante belonged to the Guelfs, who were victorious in Florence. He came of a wealthy and respected family and his career therefore seemed to be assured. But I have already recorded that the Guelfs split into two factions, the Whites and the Blacks, and the Whites, of whom Dante was one – according to gossip, only because his wife, from whom he was separated, was Black – were on the losing side. He was exiled for life, and spent 19 of his 56 years moving from place to place, expressing in his poetry his bitterness and his sorrow because he could not return to his beloved Florence. There must be as many castles in Italy in which Dante spent part of his exile as there are beds in England in which Queen Elizabeth is said to have slept.

It is quite certain that Dante spent a good deal of time in the Casentino valley as guest of the Guido family who, in the twelfth century, were lords of most of Tuscany and who, in the fourteenth, still owned the Casentino valley. They are said at one time to have owned 500 castles in Tuscany and Romagna. The ruined tower of one of these castles, the Castello di Porciano, stands on a hilltop at the northern end of the valley, some 30 miles east of Florence, and it was from here that Dante wrote one of his most famous letters – to the Emperor Henry VII. Henry had come down into Italy to try to enforce peace, and Dante urged him to 'hew the rebellious Florentines, like Agag, in pieces before the Lord'. Henry accepted this advice with notable reluctance, for he knew the strength of the Florentine army; in any case he died with Florence still uncaptured, and he is buried in Pisa cathedral. One Count Alberto Guido of Porciano earned the hostility of the Florentines by forcing their ambassador to swallow a summons ordering him to appear before the Signoria.

The most attractive town in the Casentino is undoubtedly Poppi, which has a splendid Guido castle, from which the Palazzo della Signoria in Florence was copied. From the castle walls, one looks down on the battlefield of Campaldino, where Dante is said to have fought on the side of the Guelfs. Part of the castle was built in 1191, when Guido Guerra, the first Count of Poppi, became lord of all Tuscany. One of his descendants, Count Guidoguerra IV, divided his many castles equally between his five sons. They were a quarrelsome family (which fully justified the '*guerra*' they had added to their name) and the leader of the Guelf army at Campaldino was a Guido, as was also the leader of the Ghibellines. Inside the courtyard at Poppi there is a most attractive staircase that may remind you of one of the most beautiful staircases in the world – that of the Bargello museum, in Florence. To reach the castle, you walk up a pleasantly-arcaded street and past a small chapel dedicated to the Madonna of the Plague, because a priest checked the advance in Poppi of this epidemic, that killed so many millions in the Middle Ages, by carrying an image of the Virgin through the streets.

The road back to Florence from this pleasant Casentino (the name comes from the Latin 'Clausentium' suggesting a closed-in valley) climbs up over the Consuma Pass. This pass is only a little over 1,000 metres high, but the view back down the valley to the proud tower of Poppi some 30 kilometres away is superb, especially when autumn turns to gold the forest-covered hills. The road down from the pass takes one within a few kilometres of Vallombrosa, where the autumnal leaves still 'strow the brooks', as in the days of Milton, but the scenery is radically changed by all the holiday-makers in summer and the ski-ers in winter.

9. Florence to Urbino

From Florence, most motorists follow the *Autostrada del Sole*, either northwards to Bologna or southwards towards Rome. But there are attractive alternatives. The north-bound traveller for example, can take the road to Ravenna by way of Pontassieve (where so much of the Chianti you drink, or would like to drink, is put into those attractive flasks – now, alas, much less attractive, since the straw around them is generally replaced by plastic). From Pontassieve, there are two roads to Ravenna. One, via Forlì, goes up the rich valley of the Sieve and then climbs over the Apennine pass of the Muraglione. High up in the mountains, the road forks, and one branch leads to Forlì by way of an ugly little town called Predappio, notable only for the fact that it was the birthplace of Mussolini.

His house has wisely been taken over by the Government, so nobody can make of it a source of financial or political profit. I could not decide whether the quiet and pleasant little tenant who invited us to look over it had shared any of the views expressed so forcefully by his notorious predecessor; he certainly had none of the blustering qualities one associates with Fascism, but almost the only decoration on the wall of the very poor bedroom was a poem written by some previous visitor in praise of the great Benito. There is no tablet on the outside wall of the house, or of that part of it in which the Mussolini family lived (the father, a blacksmith, working on the ground floor; the mother, a former school teacher, fighting against poverty in the drab rooms on the first floor) but the few Predappians to whom I spoke were very ready to point the place out to us. I left the town wondering whether even its most humble and liberal-minded inhabitant could remain uninfluenced by the reflected glory, resulting from the enquiries by so many visitors about their fellow-townsman who had exchanged prison cells, in which he had been shut up as a young vagrant, for the middle-age glories of the Palazzo Venezia in Rome.

The other and little-known road to Ravenna from Pontassieve takes one back through the Casentino as far as Bibbiena, and then across range after range of mountains, through Pieve Santo Stefano to Rimini. I was fascinated by this road for three reasons. One, most of it is through country so wild and thinly populated that one can scarcely believe the crowded streets of Florence are so near on one side and the crowded beachs of Rimini so near on the other. Two, the road passes near the fortress of St Leo, rebuilt in the fifteenth century by Federigo da Montefeltro on the very edge of a formidable precipice. Three, the road passes within a few miles of the Republic of San Marino.

Federigo da Montefeltro, Duke of Urbino, was one of the most famous of the condottieri and, at the same time, one of the greatest patrons of the arts. (We shall come to Urbino later.) San Leo is a stern reminder of the military side of Federigo's fantastic career. It was used as a prison even during the last century but its most notorious prisoner was the eighteenth-century alchemist and adventurer, who called himself Count Alessandro Cagliostro and who won fame throughout Europe by turning (or, rather, failing to turn) base metals into gold, by selling elixirs of youth, by claiming to be thousands of years old and by other tricks to relieve snobs and fools of their money. One of his several prisons was the Fleet, in London.

San Marino, dramatically protected by three fortresses, perched on the edge of a jagged and precipitous mountain, Monte Titano, 14 kilometres from the Adriatic, is well worth a visit. For one thing, its situation is superb, for another, this, the smallest republic in the world, (Andorra, 465 square kilometres, Liechtenstein 158, San Marino 61) has maintained its independence and its democratic form of government almost unchanged since A.D. 885, despite the ambitions of popes and of the Malatesta and Montefeltro families. Napoleon, in his republican days, was so impressed to find this small republic when he invaded Italy that he offered to enlarge its territories – an offer which the Sammarinesi tactfully refused. During the last war, when thousands of Italians from Rimini and elsewhere took refuge in this tiny neutral state, the British dropped 243 bombs on its territory, but subsequently paid compensation for the damage they had caused and, in a Declaration of Homage, paid tribute to the efforts of the Sammarinesi to maintain their neutrality. The republic is governed by two *Capitani Reggenti*, elected twice a year from the 60 members of the Grand Council, (20 for the nobility, 20 for the landowners and 20 for the burghers).

Admittedly, the Sammarinesi have nothing to learn about the importance of the tourists. The Civic Guards, increased in 1957 during a rare period of political unrest from 60 to 120, wear colourful uniforms of an earlier century. Since 1877, the Republic has issued its own postage stamps, which bring in a lot of money to the Government and also to the vendors of postcards on which to stick them. Most of the shops and cafés concentrate their attention on Germans, but there are also promises of fish and chips or 'tea as Grandma made it' or, in one case I noticed, 'English tea and toasted butter'. A less harmless way of raising funds is the sale of honours, and there must be several people in different parts of the world whose grandiose titles are the result of some financial act of calculated benevolence on Monte Titano. San Marino is said to have been founded by a stone-cutter from Dalmatia who took refuge on this mountain from the persecution of Christians by Emperor Diocletian, shortly before another emperor, Constantine, himself chose Christianity. The stone-cutter would be surprised today!

*   *   *

In common with most Italian seaside resorts, Rimini, which one can see from San Marino, consists of two towns, one very old and one very modern: one beautiful and one ugly: one now well away from the sea and one stretching along a wide but overcrowded beach, in front of a sea so shallow that it could not alarm even the most timid child. Rows upon rows of pink bodies laid out on deck-chairs under coloured umbrellas. Most of the bodies are foreign, all the houses are Italian. Very few in either category are beautiful. I am glad that the foreigners are able to enjoy a sunshine they rarely experience at home and that the Italians are able to earn a lot of money out of their enjoyment, but I am humbly grateful that this does not have to be my Italy.

The old town of Rimini is a very different matter. It existed at the time of the Etruscans, and two great Roman roads, the Via Emilia and the Via Flaminia, met here. There is a fine arch, erected in 27 B.C. when Augustus was emperor in Rome, and also a bridge, still carrying the heaviest traffic but built during the reign of Tiberius, some 50 years later. The Flaminia, built 220 years before Christ, went from Rome by way of Rieti, Spoleto, Foligno, Fossombrone to the sea at Fano. It then turned up the coast to Rimini, and here it met the Via Emilia, dating back to 187 B.C., which was the first great Roman road that did not start from Rome. It went for most of the way in a fantastically straight line to Piacenza, one of the stopping places on the present *autostrada* between Milan and Bologna. It was later extended and developed, one branch going as far as Aosta, through which one passes on the way to the Mont Blanc and Great St Bernard tunnels, and another branch going to Aquileia, between Venice and Trieste. Italian reputation for road-building does not date from yesterday.

But Rimini is memorable less for its Roman roads than for the Malatesta family that ruled it in the fourteenth and fifteenth centuries. Dante made famous the tragic love story of Paolo and Francesca, the one the brother and the other the wife of Giovanni Malatesta (*Lo Sciancato* – the lop-sided one) who

murdered them both in 1288. But the most notorious of the
Malatesta was Sigismondo, one of the most puzzling figures in
an unparalleled period of eccentrics. Among his crimes,
or alleged crimes, were these – he poisoned his first wife,
strangled the second, committed sodomy with his son and incest
with his daughters, and dedicated one of the most beautiful
churches of the early Renaissance to his favourite mistress,
Isotta degli Atti (whom he married as his third wife). The
church, officially known as San Francesco but much more frequently called the Tempio Malatestiano, was built in the
thirteenth century, but completely altered by Sigismondo in the
middle of the fifteenth. Wherever one looks, one sees the en-
twined initials of Isotta and Sigismondo, the Malatesta coat-of-
arms with an elephant and a rose, and the least solemn and
most earthly little cherubs – cupids rather than angels – I have
seen in any church. Christianity is little in evidence in this
allegedly Christian temple. In the *santuario* on the right, there
is a beautiful but much-damaged fresco by Piero della Francesca
of Sigismondo kneeling at the feet of his patron saint, but
Piero must surely have painted it with his tongue in his cheek
for the rest of the church so glorifies Sigismondo Malatesta, and
there was certainly nothing saintly about him.

Pope Pius II, who publicly condemned him to hell as 'comrade
of the devils and the damned', was himself no saint, at least
during the first half of his life. At the age of 40, after writing an
immoral play and a Boccaccio-type novel, he took holy orders,
having decided to 'forsake Venus for Bacchus', partly, he explained in his very frank memoirs, because he had had enough
of women and partly because he would find more opportunities
of advancement in the Church than outside it. Intellectually,
he was one of the greatest popes, and he seems to have been
genuinely changed by the Turkish capture of Constantinople;
he spent the latter part of his life trying to organise an outdated
Crusade, which he proposed to lead himself. (He got as far as
Ancona, but died there of fever and gout.)

He might justifiably have been indignant against Sigismondo

both for his immorality and for his blasphemy – the inscription on Isotta's tomb declares it to be 'sacred to the deified Isotta' – and there can be no doubt that Sigismondo was abominably cruel as a condottiere. But one wonders why Pius went so far as to claim that 'of all men who have ever lived, or ever will live, he was the worst ruffian, the shame of Italy and the infamy of our times'. A life-sized effigy of Sigismondo, with a placard announcing that he was 'king of traitors, hated of God and man, condemned to the flames by the vote of the holy senate', was burned on the piazza in front of St Peter's in Rome. Also one wonders about Sigismondo himself: despite his crimes and his cruelty, was a great patron of art and learning; along the outside wall of this same Tempio Malatestiano are the tombs of poets and scholars whom he had invited to Rimini.

One very attractive feature of Rimini is the canal, with its colourful fishing fleet. There is a small chapel on the canal bank to mark the spot where St Anthony once preached to the fishes because the people were too preoccupied to listen to him.

Between Rimini and Ravenna, there is very little to attract one's attention. Even one of the most famous rivers in history would fail to do so were it not for the fact that one or two enterprising 'campings' have brought the word 'Rubicon' into their names. The Rubicon is a very insignificant stream that flows into the sea about 16 kilometres north of Rimini. It once marked the frontier between Italy and Cisalpine Gaul which was part of the territory governed by Julius Caesar. By crossing it in 49 B.C., in defiance of the Roman Senate, he made his successful bid to become ruler of all Rome's immense dominions. Also his act was the origin of two phrases that survive to this day in most European languages – when he 'crossed the Rubicon', he is alleged to have exclaimed '*Alea jacta est*' – 'The die is cast.'

Unless one is pressed for time, one might do well to add an extra ten miles to one's drive to Ravenna by going inland to Cesena, where there is a Malatesta castle and a perfectly-preserved fifteenth century library. It is an ancient town that suf-

21 *Perugia: carved panels on the fountain*
22 *Perugia: the Palazzo dei Priori and the fountain*

fered severely during the struggles between the Montefeltro (who were Ghibellines) and the Malatesta (who were Guelfs). One disadvantage of a detour via Cesena is that the variety of valuable manuscripts in the library is likely to upset one's time-table.

Of Ravenna, with more accuracy than one intended, one might remark that 'it is out of this world'. It was the capital of the Roman Empire during that Empire's last few years, and yet it is outside the world of Rome. Standing in the church of San Vitale, one can more easily imagine oneself in Constantinople than in Italy. It became a Roman '*municipium*' as far back as 89 B.C., and Caesar's great-nephew, Octavianus Augustus, ordered the enlargement of its port, Classis, so that it could shelter as many as 250 ships for the defence of the Upper Adriatic, and yet for centuries it belonged more to the Eastern world than to the West.

In the opening chapter, I recalled how the Emperor Constantine divided the Roman Empire in two, and established himself in the eastern half of it, in Constantinople. His successors in the Western Empire lived, first, in Milan and, when the menace of invaders from the other side of the Alps became too acute, in Ravenna, which had two advantages. One was that much of the city was built – as Venice was later to be built – on piles, and the surrounding marshes and lagoons made it relatively easy to defend. The other was that, until the split between the Western and the Eastern Empires degenerated into open hostility after the death of Theodosius the Great in 395, the Western emperors could expect help to reach Ravenna by sea from Constantinople.

The first emperor who fled to Ravenna for these reasons was a weakling son of Theodosius named Honorius, and he was joined by his half-sister, Galla Placidia, of whom nobody would use such an adjective as 'weakling'. She had been captured by Alaric the Goth when he sacked Rome in 410 and, after his death in Southern Italy, she scandalised Roman society and her family by marrying his brother-in-law. He was murdered in

23   *Assisi: the Roman Temple of Minerva, now a church, and the Torre del Popolo*

Spain, and his widow, still young and beautiful, married again. This time her husband was Constantius, one of Honorius's generals. He died, but she planned to settle in Ravenna with their infant son, who later became Emperor Valentinian III. But her half-brother, Honorius, made such blatant love to her that there were riots in the streets of Ravenna, and she had to retire to Constantinople. Only after her half-brother's death could she return to Ravenna, where she spent the rest of her life, ruling, in all but name, what was left of the Western Empire. Her tomb is, I think, by far the greatest attraction of Ravenna.

I happen to be an admirer, but not a lover, of mosaics. I admire the skill and the patience with which the little cubes of coloured glass are selected, but I do not like the stylised saints that result from all this careful process of selection. This same defect on my part – a serious one for anybody who lives in Italy – makes it difficult for me to feel enthusiastic about the early Primitives. It is from Giotto onwards that my admiration for Italian art turns to affection.

But this little mausoleum of Galla Placidia is unique. For one thing, no other mosaics I have ever seen have deep, rich blues and greens to compare with those of this tomb. For another thing, these mosaics are the oldest in Ravenna and paradoxically it was the later mosaics that became impossibly stylised – it was Constantinople that produced the stiff figures that are still so notable a feature of the Orthodox Church. But the Galla Placidia mosaics date from the fifth century and still were more influenced by Greek and Roman ideas.

The mausoleum is dark, despite its alabaster windows which give a subdued, golden light far more beautiful than any stained glass, so it is best to go there when there is strong sunshine outside. Most guidebooks seem to advise tourists first to visit the basilica of San Vitale, the door of which one passes on the way to the Galla Placidia tomb. I disagree, since the mausoleum was built a century before the basilica, San Vitale is much more like a mosque than a Christian church and, being circular, bears little resemblance to the normal and severe basilica, which consists of a nave, flanked by aisles but generally without the transepts that give the building the shape of a cross. (A 'basilica', in its literal sense, is a royal building, but it came to mean either a public hall or a church.)

The Galla Placidia temple is cruciform, and is built of the dull red brick one finds in most of Ravenna's churches (since the land on which the city is built consists entirely of sand). The exterior, with its blind arches, is dignified and impressive, but it gives no hint of the splendour of the interior, where the central dome is so startling a feature that one has the impression of being in a circular building. One does not, at first, even notice the three chapels with the sarcophagus of Galla Placdia facing the doorway and, allegedly, those of her half-brother, Honorius, on the right and of her second husband, Constantius, on the left. One sees only the intense blue, shot with gold, of the night sky, which is the dome. (Note how the arrangement of the stars and the deepening blue of the sky combine to emphasise the infinite distance of the cross at the apex of the dome.)

One endearing feature of the mosaics in the Ravenna churches is the importance given to animals. In the lunette above the entrance of the Galla Placidia tomb, a beardless Christ sits surrounded by his sheep; in the two transverse lunettes, stags approach a pool. In other and later Ravenna mosaics, animals are still more prominent but are arranged with much less informality. The Good Shepherd motif, for example, recurs in both Sant' Apollinare Nuovo and in Sant' Apollinare in Classe, but they serve to emphasise the contrast between the Romano-Hellenistic effort to represent God as a human being and the Byzantine effort to lift the human being towards the level of God by taking the vitality away from the human face and form.

The two schools of artistic and religious thought are present in the mosaics of nearby San Vitale, but one at first scarcely notices the mosaics; one is so astonished by the impression that here, on Italian soil and under the control of the Catholic Church in Rome, is a Byzantine temple, the like of which could not be found anywhere else in Western Europe, except, perhaps, in a Greek or Russian Orthodox church. Eastern, even to the lotus leaves – so common in the East but so rare in the West – which decorate the capitals of some of the columns.

The mosaics seem to me to lack the glorious depth of those of the Placidia temple, but possibly this would not be my impression had I first visited San Vitale. The pale greens of the lunette showing two incidents in the life of Abraham are lovely; the little ram that has suddenly arrived at the feet of Abraham so that he need not sacrifice his son is so charming that one feels God must have intervened also on its behalf. St Mark's lion is splendidly ferocious. Christ, seated on the globe and nonchalantly handing the crown of martyrdom to St Vitale, is again portrayed without a beard as, indeed, are most of the priests and courtiers accompanying the Emperor Theodosius. (The portrait of Archbishop Maximianus, on the Emperor's immediate left, must be one of the most successful and accurate portraits ever made in mosaic.)

The mosaics are so splendid that one might not notice the very exceptional marbles that cover the pilasters – the most delicately-coloured of any I know. Nor should one miss the sculptures on the sarcophagus of the Exarch Isaccio in the chapel on the right of the apse. He died in the seventh century, but experts claim that these carvings were done well over two centuries earlier. The Three Holy Kings, bringing their gifts, bear no resemblance to the three elderly, tired and bearded gentlemen most of us have in mind – they appear to be in their early 20s, and to be running to fulfil their good mission. There is also a young person in a Phrygian cap, with two tame lions, who look as though they were waiting to be rewarded with a dog-biscuit apiece.

After my visits to the tomb of Galla Placidia and the basilica of San Vitale, I hurried back to the *Italianità* of the Piazza del Popolo, one of the most charming squares I know. But even the Piazza del Popolo is different from other busy squares in other parts of Italy – it was so obviously influenced by Venice, and Venice was so obviously influenced by the East.

Sant' Apollinare Nuovo (which is not very new, since it was built in the first quarter of the sixth century) and the very similar Sant' Apollinare in Classe (Classis, a mile or two to the south, being the ancient port) are both very remarkable for their mosaics. The former is memorable above all for its procession, along one side of the building, of 22 virgins, preceded by three youthful Holy Kings, in as great a hurry as those on the sarcophagus in St Vitale to pay homage to Mary and her infant son. On the other side of the basilica is a similar procession of 26 male saints approaching Christ with wreaths. In this basilica Christ is portrayed in one place with a beard and in another clean-shaven, and one is tempted to conclude that, since most Roman sculptured heads are clean-shaven, the bearded Christ was introduced from Byzantium. This, however, is not so: my learned friend, Professor Michael Grant, had no difficulty in naming three bearded Christs in the Catacombs of Rome, carved well before the building of Constantinople. Apparently the idea of Christ with a beard came from Syria and Palestine in the very early days of Christianity. On the right-hand wall of this church there is a group of the principal buildings of Ravenna; the similar space on the left is given up to an interesting representation of the port of Classis in Roman times, with ships and two lighthouse towers. The coffered ceiling of the seventeenth century would be magnificent in some churches; here it seems to me disturbingly out of place.

Sant' Apollinare in Classe is younger than Sant' Apollinare Nuovo by some 20 years. I find it very much more impressive. In Galla Placidia's tomb, the alabaster windows give only a diffused light which is nevertheless sufficient to reveal the fantastic depths of the blues and greens; here the alabaster windows let in much more light to reveal the delicate shades of the superb marble columns, believed to have come from the East, and to increase the cheerfulness of the basilica's most attractive feature – the mosaic in the bowl of the apse, high above the altar. (Much of the marble panelling was stripped away in 1449 by

Sigismondo Malatesta for the benefit of his Tempio Malatestiano in Rimini.)

The main feature of the apse is the mosaic of St Apollinare against a background of restful green and beneath a large circle of darker green, filled with a cross and golden stars. In the centre of the cross is a small head of Christ. This mosaic is attractive above all on account of the birds, trees and flowers with which the green background is dotted, and for the sheep which stand, with military precision, on either side of the saint. (Only the birds are informal.) Both these churches have tall round towers of pale brick. They might therefore, look like factory chimneys; for some reason I cannot define, they are beautiful.

There are, of course, several other buildings that add to Ravenna's immense attraction. Two I had long wanted to see disappointed me – the mausoleum of Theodoric and the tomb of Dante. As recorded in my first chapter, Theodoric, leader of the Ostrogoths, invaded Italy in 489, defeated Odoacer (or Odovakar or Ottokar), a former 'barbarian' officer in the Imperial army, and removed him as a possible rival by murdering him at dinner in Ravenna. But thereafter Theodoric ruled Italy so well for 33 years that he merited the title of 'the Great'. His tomb is on the eastern outskirts of Ravenna – an enormous round affair, with a roof which consists of a single slab of stone weighing at least three hundred tons, brought from the other side of the Adriatic. Noteworthy, but not beautiful. And I am sorry to say that I could use the same adjectives about Dante's tomb, although I should also add the word 'dignified'. Dante's last home was in Ravenna, where he was greatly honoured. It was on behalf of Ravenna that he went on a diplomatic mission to Venice, and he died in 1321 of a fever caught in the marshes between the two towns. Ravenna has therefore always refused to send back his remains to Florence, which had driven him into exile.

Near Dante's tomb is the church of San Francesco, which would merit a star in a guidebook to most other cities. In its crypt the original pavement lies under several feet of water. I have already mentioned that Ravenna was built originally on piles, as is Venice today. The River Po in the course of ages has brought down so much silt and the marshes have been so carefully drained that the sea has now receded some five miles or so. But the water level has not sunk much, whereas the buildings have. Even inside St Vitale there is a kind of bath from which the water has regularly to be pumped out to prevent the whole floor from being flooded, and the floors of many old buildings have had to be raised. This strikes me as remarkable, but that adjective applies to so much in Ravenna. Even had he not been involved in his last major love affair, with the Countess Teresa Guiccioli, Byron might still have decided that he found Ravenna more interesting and attractive than any other Italian city. Even in his day, there could not have been many towns with pinewoods so spacious but so unfrequented that he could practise pistol-shooting in them.

Ravenna is my northernmost limit. As I explained in the first chapter, I have included it in this book mainly because so many visitors to the Adriatic coast of Central Italy push northwards as far as this city, whereas it is well away from the beaten track for visitors to the other cities of Northern Italy.

From Ravenna, we drove back along the coast to Pesaro, where we turned inland to visit Urbino. The artistic reputation of Urbino is perhaps even more the work of one man than is the artistic reputation of Florence, and one needs to remember that it is a small town of about 7,000 inhabitants, situated 450 metres up in hills which soon develop, as one goes west towards larger centres of civilisation, into ranges of great mountains. This wild and almost deserted country is the country of the Montefeltro, and it is very different from Florence, the undisputed birthplace of the Renaissance. And yet Federigo da Montefeltro attracted almost every famous artist of his day to Urbino. Like Lorenzo de' Medici, he mixed display with democracy, and liked to stroll among his people in the streets of Urbino, chatting to them and listening to their grievances.

Seldom was a ruler more genuinely beloved.

Urbino was an important, fortified hill town long before the Montefeltro family acquired control of it in the twelfth century. It was in the fifteenth that Federigo who, like so many young men of famous families, had been a successful condottiere, selling his services and those of his little army to the highest bidder, settled down to rule his duchy. He had strengthened his position by marrying Battista Sforza, member of the ruling family in nearby Pesaro, and by agreeing to his daughter's marriage to Giovanni della Rovere, favourite nephew of Pope Sixtus IV. Nor was this all, for his only son, Guidobaldo, married Elizabeth Gonzaga, of the ruling family in Mantua.

Even with these valuable family connections, life was uncertain. Guidobaldo was turned out of the Duchy in 1497 by Caesar Borgia, 'nephew' (euphemism for 'son') of Pope Alexander VI, but he returned to Urbino in 1503. After his death five years later, the immense dukedom went to a member of the della Rovere family, Francesco Maria, as strong and violent as Guidobaldo had been delicate and gentle. He murdered a cardinal in a street in Ravenna, stabbed his sister's lover in Urbino, and knocked down Italy's greatest historian, Francesco Guicciardini, at a meeting. (The pen being mightier than the sword, Guiccciardini got his own back.) But he was a fine soldier. The last Duke of Urbino died in 1624, and thereafter the Duchy was one of the Papal States until Italy became united and independent in 1870.

Piero della Francesca's portrait of Federigo must be one of the most famous and fascinating portraits in the world. Apart from its composition – rich red cap and cloak, extraordinary dark hair, and pale distant landscape – the man's face draws your attention. He had broken his nose and lost his right eye in a military tournament, and was therefore always portrayed in profile. The broken nose adds to his imperious look, already suggested by the long upper lip and the determined chin. But the eye suggests immense intelligence, and also a slightly melancholic calm. The portrait of a man who had deserved and won a high place in the world, but who was left with few illusions. (This portrait, and Piero's companion portrait of Federigo's wife, Battista Sforza, are in the Uffizi in Florence.)

Guidobaldo was sickly and lacked his father's determination but he, too (helped very much by his beautiful and intelligent wife) made his contribution to the fame of the court at Urbino. Henry VII of England made him a Knight of the Garter, and in return Guidobaldo sent the English king a small painting by Raphael of 'St George and the Dragon', now in the Louvre. The envoy who took this gift to England was Baldassare Castiglione, author of *Il Libro del Cortegiano*, the most famous book ever written on how the aristocratic young courtier ought to behave. He must have produced a great many intolerable young snobs, for his book was translated into many languages. (Consulting it recently in connection with another book I was writing, I copied down his advice that the young courtier should know 'how to swim, jump, run, throw stones; for, besides their usefulness in war, it is frequently necessary to show one's prowess in such things, whereby a good name is to be won, especially with the crowd, with whom one must reckon, after all. Another noble exercise, and most suitable for a man at court, is the game of tennis, which shows off the disposition of the body, the quickness and litheness of every member, and all the qualities that are brought out by almost every other form of exercise.') I find it interesting that the court upon which this book on gentlemanly behaviour was based should have been that of the small and remote city of Urbino.

There was no need for Federigo to hold out special attractions to two of the most famous artists of the time, Raphael the painter and Bramante the architect, for they were natives of Urbino. The house in which Raphael was born is well worth a visit, for it has been well restored and equipped with good period furniture. Raphael's father, Giovanni Santi, was himself an artist of considerable merit, and several of his paintings hang in the Ducal Palace. The ground floor of his house was a shop in which he sold his own works and those of other artists; it is still used as an artists' centre, and when I visited it the walls were covered by Pop Art posters, strongly contrasting with the pictures in the rest of the house – with, for example, Giovanni Santi's 'Madonna and Child' in Raphael's bedroom. (The Madonna in this picture is said to be Raphael's mother, who died when he was very young.)

Some people find Urbino sad, inasmuch as it so obviously lives in the past, and I notice that two of the longest streets have names that are not exactly cheerful – *'Via Giro dei Debitori'* or 'Debtors' Walk' and *'Via dei Morti'* or 'Street of the Dead'. 'Every sort of scholar came to Urbino,' wrote Edward Hutton in his *The Cities of Umbria* (Methuen, London, 1905), 'great poets, painters, sculptors, architects, engineers, doctors, priests, quacks of every kind, fools and nobles, dancing masters and beautiful women, musicians and preachers flocked to the court of one of the most humane princes Italy had ever seen'. But one climbs up the hilly streets looking in vain at least for some tablet to announce where so-and-so lived in the great days. The house of Raphael, yes, but that is all.

And yet I drove out of the city gate and down the hill in a mood almost of elation – this return to small town provincialism serves to emphasise the greatness of the man who once made it so famous, a man who was a great soldier, but who is remembered not on account of his valour but on account of his civilised ideas and ideals. The popes took his great library to Rome, and many of the pictures that formerly hung on the palace walls have found their way to the picture galleries of Europe. And yet this palace remains beautiful and gay – an adjective one would not normally apply to a building with I don't know how many scores of rooms. This is not a fortress, but a palace; not a palace with perfectly planned proportions like Versailles, but a successful amalgamation of an old castle with the relatively small building in which the Montefeltro family was living in the fifteenth century. The windows are not narrow slits made primarily for defence, but large windows to admit the sunlight. In the words of Baldassare Castiglione, 'it appeared rather a palatial city than a palace'.

From the moment one enters the quadrangular courtyard – reckoned by some experts to be the most beautiful in Italy – and begins to walk up the easy and wide treads of the staircase, one loses the feeling of visiting a museum; it may sound absurd to say so in the midst of all this grandeur, but the feeling is more that of coming into somebody's home. In the Duke's apartments, for example, there is the Room of the Angels, so-called on account of all the cheerful little cherubs – angels? – prancing around as the decorations of the huge chimney-piece; they destroy any sense of solemnity such as one might be expected to feel in all this splendour.

The most revealing part of the palace is the Duke's chapel, reached by an extraordinary spiral staircase in the tower (300 steps with no central core). The chapel is in two parts, 'one sacred to God, the other to the Muses', a very characteristic blending of orthodox religion and humanistic aspirations. The Duke's study contains what is probably the world's richest display of *intarsio*, or wood inlay – also to be noted in several of the doors in the palace – some of which also include examples of *trompe l'oeil*. There are bookshelves, open cupboards, musical instruments, flowers and so on which, in fact, are not there at all, except as pictures made of very skilful inlays of different-coloured woods.

Between the two towers are balconies with views towards the plain and the sea. From one of these balconies, Guidobaldo II, grandson of the Guidobaldo who shares with Federigo the credit for the great days of Urbino, watched for the arrival of his future wife, Vittoria Farnese. Seeing in the distance the dust stirred up by the horses of her approaching cavalcade, he scratched, in Latin, this rather pathetic little announcement on the wall: 'In 1548, at 21 hours, the Duke saw his wife; may her coming be happy and last for ever.'

10. The Apennines and the Adriatic

The visitor to Urbino should think a little about geography before making his next move. In Ravenna and Rimini, he was on the southern edge of the great plain of the River Po, widening as it stretches eastwards to the Adriatic. Should he have wished to return to Central Italy, he could have driven along straight, flat roads as far as Bologna, and then have crossed the Apennines by the easy and elegant *Autostrada del Sole* to Florence. But at Urbino he is already far enough south of this plain to be involved in the lower slopes of the Apennines. His easiest way westwards is now along the Via Flaminia, through the gorge of the Furlo Pass.

But this will be his last chance of seeing something more of Italy east of the Apennines, Italy between the mountains and the Adriatic. There are, of course, other roads across the mountains, but none so easy as the Via Flaminia, for the Apennines get higher and wider as they go south, until they culminate in the Gran Sasso d'Italia (more than 2,600 metres, or 9,500 feet) and the wildness of the Abruzzi. He may be discouraged because there will be few towns farther south whose names are familiar to him. Besides, the long, flat beaches attract buildings that are ugly, and the map will show him that the hinterland consists of scores of very steep mountains and very deep valleys. Most of the roads marked on it would take him through magnificent mountain scenery and past small and ancient towns which would fill him with admiration for the toughness of the Italians who live in them. But this is not tourist country – not yet, at any rate. The Apennines are best explored from the Umbrian side, that is, from the west. Even this is difficult, although the elaborate fortifications of some of the little towns indicate their past importance.

(One is apt to forget that, until the invention of the internal combustion engine, almost every town was, by modern standards, appallingly remote. When one travelled on horseback or in a jolting and creaking coach, the distance one could cover in a day depended upon the strength of one's horses, not upon the power of one's car. With the building of each new tunnel and the straightening out of each old bend in the road, the temptation to use only the main roads becomes stronger, and the busy little agricultural towns, so valuable for a nation's economy, become more 'quaint'. But not yet quaint enough to have guide books written about them.)

I imagine, therefore, that most visitors to Urbino will decide that they cannot afford the time to explore such little-known country, and will follow the Via Flamina to Florence or Perugia or some other city that they already know well, if only by repute. But some will want to see a little more of Italy east of the Apennines. This is so mountainous a region that I have selected only a few towns that are easy to reach from larger towns with good accommodation. They would do well, for example, to make Ancona their headquarters for excursions to three of them – Loreto, Macerata and Jesi.

Of these three, Loreto alone could claim to be famous, at least among Catholics. It is a sanctuary almost as frequented as Lourdes, although much less accessible. Pilgrims arrive there by thousands, especially on any kind of festival linked with the name of the Virgin Mary. Pope John XXIII emphasised its importance by going there on his first journey away from Rome. For at Loreto there is a small brick building, about nine metres long, four metres wide and four metres high, which is alleged to be the house of the Virgin Mary, transported by angels from

Nazareth and set down, in 1294, among the laurels that give Loreto its name. Owing to this miraculous flight, the Madonna of Loreto is the patron saint of aviators. As, alas, is so common in such sanctuaries, any stimulus to meditation on the humility of a Holy Family that has had so great an influence on the history of mankind is checked by the demonstrative splendour of the works of art that surround the Holy House. They justify a visit more from the artistic than from the religious point of view. This little house stands under the dome of a large church, the building of which ws begun in 1468 and to which some of the greatest artists and architects of the time contributed – Antonio da Sangallo, Bramante, Luca Signorelli, Melozzo da Forlì, Sansovino and Guiliano da Maiano among them. Once again, one is filled with amazement and admiration for the industry and the ubiquity of the artists of the Renaissance. If there were fewer and less persistent sellers of rosaries and holy images in the streets, one would be in a better mood to appreciate these works of art and their setting in this little town, with its sixteenth-century walls and bastions, and the apse of its church, surprisingly but splendidly battlemented.

Seven kilometres north of Loreto is Castelfidardo, where one of the most significant battles in the history of Italy was fought, in the autumn of 1860. A few months earlier, Garibaldi had carried out his fantastically successful invasion of Sicily and southern Italy. He was in Naples, preparing to attack the papal troops in order to occupy Rome and, very possibly, playing with the idea of himself becoming president of a Republic of Southern Italy. To Cavour and his master, King Victor Emanuel of Savoy, either alternative would have been disastrous. Italy was far too weak to face the international consequences of the expulsion from Rome of a pope who was defended by French troops, and Garibaldi as president in southern Italy would very probably have postponed for years any hope of a united Italy and certainly would have destroyed Victor Emanuel's hope of being its king. It was essential that Victor Emanuel's forces should join up with Garibaldi's victorious legionaries without delay. The world must see that Garibaldi, Cavour and Mazzini, such unexpected allies during the efforts to unite their country, were still allies in this moment of success.

But that meant that the King and his Piedmontese troops must themselves face the papal forces, and invade papal territory. This they did on a rather slender excuse, and in September the Piedmontese won a decisive victory at Castelfidardo; the King and Garibaldi had a dramatic meeting a few miles north of Naples; they rode into the city side by side, with Garibaldi calling on the Neopolitans to welcome their king; and Garibaldi then withdrew to the obscurity of his little farm on the island of Caprera, just off the northern tip of Sardinia. One wonders what would have been the outcome for Italy had the papal troops won a victory at Castelfidardo.

I do not know how much young Italians now learn about Castelfidardo, but I should not be surprised if a good many of them know less about its importance in their history than about its importance in the manufacture of accordions.

Macerata differs from most other towns reached from the Adriatic mainly in that it is larger (with some 20,000 inhabitants) and has a university. This university, in this small and remote town, is one of the 12 oldest universities in Italy – it was founded in 1290. Macerata is well placed on a hill between two valleys, and it has some good buildings. The Loggia dei Mercanti (early sixteenth century) is one of the most elegant buildings of the kind in Italy. One unusual feature is the *sferisterio*, which was built in 1829 for the game of *pallone*, very popular in this part of Italy. I find the name interesting, since the normal name for a sports ground in Italy would be *stadio*, from the Latin *stadium*; *sferisterio*, on the other hand, is taken from the Greek, and it serves as a reminder that Italy east of the Apennines has been much more closely linked with Greece and the Eastern Mediterranean than Italy west of that great spine of mountains. This becomes much more obvious, of course, in the south-eastern region of Apulia where Greeks had settled before the foundation of Rome – Otranto, near the 'heel' of Italy is only 80 kilometres from Albania and more than 600 from Rome.

The Marches also suffered more than most of Italy from invaders from the north – it was as easy for them to come down the Adriatic coast as it was difficult for them to cross the Apennines into the wealthier parts of the peninsula. Macerata and the near-by little town of Recanati both owe their existence to the destruction by the Visigoths of the Roman colony of Helvia Recina (six kilometres away) in the fifth century. The Leopardi palace should be visited, especially by those at all interested in Italian literature, for one of Italy's greatest poets, Giacomo Leopardi, was born there in 1798, and its library has a fine collection of his books and manuscripts. The main road to Ancona passes the not inconsiderable ruins of Helvia Recina, and the name of Macerata is said to be taken from the word *macerie*, the rubble to which the Visigoths had reduced their former homes there.

Jesi (Iesi to the Italians who make no use of the letter j) is likely to escape your notice unless you return to the west by way of Fabriano, and not through Tolentino or, farther south, along the ancient Via Salaria. Like all these other small towns in the lower Apennines, it has its attractions, but it is of especial interest to the historian, for it is the birthplace of the Emperor Frederick ii, one of the most fascinating figures in Italian history. Even his birth was, to say the least, unusual. His father, a member of the Hohenstaufen family from Swabia in southern Germany, had married Constance, daughter of one of the Norman kings of Sicily. When Frederick was born, his mother was over 40 and had been married for nine years without having a child. Realising how people gossiped, how important the birth of her son would be to European politics, and how anxious the rivals of the Hohenstaufens would be to discredit her, she gave birth to Frederick, '*Stupor Mundi*', in a tent erected on the main square of Jesi, in the presence of 19 cardinals or bishops.

24   *Assisi: the upper church*

The infant produced in these unusual circumstances became one of the most important humanists of all time and the father of a family, partly legitimate and partly illegitimate, whom the pope condemned as 'a nest of vipers'. Should you take this road through Fabriano, you will also pass through Gualdo Tadino, where the Byzantine general, Narses, then only a septuagenarian, defeated and killed the greatest of the Goth invaders, Totila.

But before taking this, or any other road across the Apennines, the visitor will have visited Ancona, which has one of the few fine natural harbours along the Italian Adriatic coast. It was founded some 400 years before Christ by the Doric Greeks, and its name comes from the Greek for 'elbow'. Despite the fact that it is on Italy's east coast and there is a fine panoramic road along its eastern cliff, the port faces west. Thus it can claim to be the only Italian town from which one can see sunrise and sunset over the sea. High on the promontory between the harbour and the open sea is the Duomo, built in the twelfth century on the ruins of a temple to Venus, ten columns from which are in the cathedral. This Duomo has a simple and dignified façade with an unexpectedly large, but outstandingly beautiful, porch, the front columns of which are supported by two lions, such as the Comacine masons carved for so many churches in northern Tuscany. Next to the cathedral is the episcopal palace, where Pope Pius II – whose name appears several times in this book – died while he was organising his crusade against the Turks.

The harbour is naturally so good that Ancona must have been an important place even in pre-Roman times. It is widely accepted that the Etruscans may have come, in small numbers and over a long period, from Asia Minor, but the Piceni, the people of this Adriatic coast, seem to be the autochthonous inhabitants. There was, of course, an infiltration of Greeks from the south and of Gauls, Veneti and others from the north but the Piceni were here, as the Umbrians were on the other side of the Apennines, at least six centuries before Christ. The Ancona museum

25 *Spoleto: the cathedral*

has an unusually good collection of pre-Roman antiquities, and one has a strange impression that here, cut off from the rest of Italy by the mountains, there is a more direct link than one would find elsewhere between these relics of the Iron Age and the people passing in the street outside (although I suppose this impression is to some extent contradicted by the discovery that every picture gallery in the area has paintings by Crivelli, Lorenzo Lotto or other Venetian painters whose pictures are very rare west of the Apennines).

At the time of Augustus, Picenum was one of the 11 regions into which Italy was divided, and at one end of the port, beneath Monte Guasco and the Duomo, there is a fine arch, erected in 113 A.D. in honour of the Emperor Trajan, who had a lot to do with the improvements to the harbour. So excellent a harbour, of course, aroused envy; Ancona had to withstand sieges by the Emperor Lothaire II in 1137, by the Emperor Frederick Barbarossa in 1167, by the Venetian fleet in 1173. After the capture of Constantinople by the Turks in 1453, Ancona lost much of its importance and its strength, and its citizens became the victims of the customary feuds between the ruling families until the papal authorities succeeded in enforcing law and order. After the battle of Castelfidardo, it was able to break away from the Papal States and to become part of the Italian kingdom. Visitors to Ancona will be fortunate if their visit coincides with the annual *Fiera della Pesca*, the Fish Fair, which takes place in July and August. In no other town and at no other time are they likely to find such a variety of creatures caught in the Mediterranean. This fair is an unusual trading occasion of international economic importance.

From Ancona, the visitor would be wise to drive to Ascoli Piceno, noticing the thirteenth-century castle at Porto San Giorgio on the way. There are also several little ports from which some fishermen still go to sea, despite the counter-attractions of the tourist industry.

Ascoli Piceno, originally a Sabine town, is a beautiful little place, built on a tongue of land where two rivers meet, and flanked by high mountains. The amount of prehistoric material in the museum proves it to be very old, but it enters into history only when the Romans captured it in 268 B.C. and later made it an important station on the Via Salaria. Asculum, as it was then known, played an important part in the so-called Social War against Rome, and its citizens massacred all the Romans inside its walls in 99 B.C. The Romans recaptured it in the following year, killed the civic leaders and exiled the rest. One interesting exhibit in the museum is a number of acorn-shaped lumps of lead, the ammunition used by slingers during this Social War. From the time of Charlemagne, it was considered important enough for its bishops to have the title of prince and to mint their own money.

There is plenty to remind one of the Romans. A fine bridge across the gorge of the River Trento is Roman and so is one of the gates, the Porta Gemina. Outside the walls – a small section of which is Roman – there are the ruins of a Roman theatre, and the Romanesque church of San Gregorio has columns from the temple of Vesta, on the ruins of which the church is built. The Duomo and the Baptistery (a square building at ground level which becomes octagonal higher up) are both built on Roman foundations. But it is Romanesque Ascoli, rather than Roman Ascoli, that is so attractive. Or rather, Romanesque and Renaissance, for several of the churches show signs of both. The Palazzo del Popolo, for example, is a very lovely Romanesque building of pink brick, but it has an imposing Renaissance doorway that was added in 1548 by Cola dell'Amatrice, an architect who was very busy in this part of the world. This mixture may be depressing to those who know a lot about architecture; to me, additions of this sort give a pleasant sense of continuity (unless they involve, say, Victorian additions to a Georgian house). I doubt if anybody could dislike the Piazza del Popolo, with its Renaissance façades, its arcades surmounted by Ghibelline merlons, its great Palazzo along one side of it and, at its end, the very unusual Gothic church of San Francesco, flanked by the

five graceful arches of the Loggia dei Mercanti – early sixteenth century. There are other churches showing Venetian,
Lombard or Tuscan influence and, most picturesque of all, a
mediaeval quarter, complete with the towers built by rich
families to show their superiority over their neighbours. If it
were easier to reach, Ascoli Piceno would undoubtedly be one
of the most famous small towns in Italy.

From Ascoli Piceno, the more adventurous will take a picturesque mountain road southwards to Teramo, and then on,
almost in the shadow of the Gran Sasso d'Italia, to L'Aquila,
reaching the western slopes of the Apennines at Rieti. But both
Teramo and L'Aquila are in the Abruzzi, the wildest and most
mountainous of Italy's 20 regions, and they are outside the
scope of this book. I must advise the traveller who has come
thus far down the Adriatic coast to cross the mountains by
way of the Via Salaria to the gentler hills of Umbria.

Then there are those other travellers – the great majority –
who, studying the map at Urbino, decide to follow the Via
Flaminia to Florence, Perugia, Rome, or whatever other city
their destination may be. And, indeed, the Via Flaminia is the
road one should take to Rome, since no other road does more
to enhance one's respect for the Ancient Romans.

It is along this road that Roman legions marched on their re-
turn from campaigns in Gaul and Britain and Central Europe.
They would have come down the coast from Rimini to Pesaro,
which was an important city even in their day. The visitor to
Pesaro in our time can admire the fine Ducal Palace, now the
Prefettura, which belonged in turn to the Sforza and the Della
Rovere, and the house where Italy's beloved composer, Gioac-
chino Rossini (1792-1868) was born. He can also visit the
museum with its display of majolica for which Pesaro, with
Faenza, Urbania (formerly Castel Durante), Gubbio and Urbino,
used to be famous.

Twelve kilometres farther south, at Fano, the Roman legionaries would have turned inland towards the mountains. Fano,

like Rimini, has its Arch of Augustus, to celebrate the building of the Via Flaminia, and one is further reminded of the importance this road had for the people by the fact that these arches are represented on the façades of the Tempio Malatestiano in Rimini and of San Michele in Fano. Very near this latter church, a small section of the not-so-modern roadway has been removed, to show large flagstones of the original Via Flaminia.

Climbing up into the Apennines, the legionaries would have passed Monte Pietralata, near which the Consuls Claudius Nero and Livius Salinator defeated Hasdrubal, coming to the help of his brother, Hannibal, in 207 B.C., and thereby wiped out the shame of the Roman defeat by Hannibal at Lake Trasimene ten years earlier. Claudius Nero, down in the heel of Italy at Taranto, had intercepted messages between the two brothers which revealed Hasdrubal's plans, and had urged the Senate in Rome to send all the soldiers they could to the Via Flaminia to trap the Phoenicians in the deep gorge of the Furlo Pass, meanwhile, he hurried his own troops up the coast to join those of Livius Salinator at Sena Gallica (now Senigallia). The Phoenician army was destroyed, Hasdrubal was killed, his head was sent to Hannibal, and Roman victory in the Second Punic War was assured.

The Furlo Pass is only some 180 metres above sea level, but the high and vertical cliffs on either side of the narrow gorge make it as impressive as the Gorges du Tarn in Southern France, and historically much more interesting. At its narrowest stretch, there is a fine example of the road-building for which Italy was and is so famous. The existing road passes through a short tunnel, constructed in A.D. 77, during the rule of the Emperor Vespasian. This is flanked by a much narrower and smaller tunnel, said to date back to 220 B.C. And between this small tunnel and the river, there is an artificial wall, built of flat stones, which is believed to have been made by the Etruscans.

One might do well to leave Via Flaminia at Schieggia, in order to visit Gubbio, famous for its annual *Corsa dei Ceri*, or Race of the Candles, which brings thousands upon thousands of visitors to the little Umbrian town every 15 May. Disliking crowds, I shall never see this ceremony, or the *Palio* in Siena, or – with the possible exception of the *Giostra del Saraceno*, the tilting tournament in Arezzo – any of the other picturesque festivals which enable the local Italians to dress up in fourteenth-century uniforms for the glory of God, for their own enjoyment and for the benefit of the tourist trade. Doubtless, I miss a lot, but I imagine the 'atmosphere of almost hysterical abandon which possesses the city on the day of the *Corsa dei Ceri*' (*Umbria* by Michael Adams, Faber, 1964) derives from the fact that for the rest of the year Gubbio is quiet, a little melancholy, living on its memories. The one festival in Gubbio I would gladly attend is on 18 May when Gubbio competes with Borgo San Sepolcro in a crossbow tournament, and this I would do because, in San Sepolcro, I was once privileged to shoot with this formidable weapon. I believe the only other towns where the crossbow – a very heavy kind of catapult fixed on a stand – attracts competitors are San Marino and, far away on the west coast of Tuscany, Massa Marittima.

The *Corsa dei Ceri* 'is not, properly speaking, a race since it makes no difference who arrives first at the finishing post', writes Michael Adams, and the 'candles' are, in fact, 'great wooden structures 20 feet high which are carried in a vertical position and at great speed by rival teams up the steep hill behind the city to the church of the patron of Gubbio, Sant' Ubaldo'. Each of the three '*ceri*' is carried by members of rival guilds and is surmounted by the emblem of a saint – St Antony for the farm-workers, St George for the merchants and St Ubaldo for the masons. Despite the saints' emblems and the blessing of the bishop, one imagines that the origin of this ancient festival was pagan. Whatever its origin, from all accounts it lets loose a passionate excitement more generally associated with Carnival than with a religious festival (which Carnival is not, since it is the last outburst of human celebration before the religious disciplines of Lent).

But Gubbio without its *ceri* is also very attractive, with a severe kind of beauty that seems to be typical of Umbria. *Campanilismo*, which is inadequately translated by 'local patriotism', is more pronounced in Umbria than in Tuscany, for reasons explained by Michael Adams in the best book on Umbria I know, and it is due rather to geography than to history. It is the only one of Italy's 18 Regions that has neither an outlet to the sea nor a frontier with a non-Italian state, and most of its territory lies at a height of more than 300 metres. Even its fertile plains, which now permit rapid progress along good roads, did not in early days provide easy movement of men and ideas from one part of the region to another, for some of these plains were lakes until the Romans drained them – the citizens of Perugia and Assisi, for example, looked out over water, instead of fields. Thus, the early Umbrians, even more than the early Tuscans, built their towns on the hill-tops, and their hill-tops are even higher than those of Tuscany. Umbria used to be smaller than it is now, and Adams argues that its people lived in the narrow area between the Apennines to the east and the Tiber to the west, with the Etruscans on the far side of this river. 'Even a foreign ear can detect the change in dialect between one side of the river and the other. Perugia, on the west bank, is Etruscan, like Todi, like Orvieto; Assisi, on the east bank, is Umbrian, like Spoleto, like Gubbio.'

These Umbrians were suspicious of the valleys, for they facilitated the arrival of all the barbarian invaders trying to reach Rome. But their isolation also led to intense distrust between one Umbrian town and another. On the other hand, this remoteness from the affairs of the outside world attracted seekers after solitude and opportunities for reflection. Towards the end of the fifth century, St Benedict was born in the remote little Umbrian town of Norcia, east of Spoleto; to the Benedictine Order which he founded, more than to any other organisation or society, goes the credit for keeping alive some respect for learning during the worst periods of the Dark Ages. St Francis was born in Assisi some seven centuries later, and has probably done more than any other mortal man to keep alive the spirit of Christianity.

Campanilismo may be more acute in Umbria than in other regions, and Heaven knows that it is strong everywhere in Italy. But it would be a mistake to conclude that Umbria was, or is, a backward region. To quote Michael Adams once more, 'by the fourteenth century, for instance, Perugia – like Pisa and Florence and Milan – enjoyed civic standards and amenities incomparably more advanced than those of Paris or Hamburg, to say nothing of London; its streets were paved, its public buildings were grandiose and elegant ... and Perugian merchants travelled all over the continent to bring back the wealth with which they embellished their city'. The weakness of Perugia, of Gubbio, of Assisi and other cities was that each was a unit on its own, frequently at war with some neighbouring unit only a few miles away, and was thus unable to defend itself successfully against any invaders, however uncultured and savage, with enough discipline to combine against the cultured and civilised who were worth looting and plundering. This jealous *campanilismo*, as I have pointed out elsewhere, has been Italy's greatest weakness, ever since the collapse of the Roman Empire, but it has probably had more disastrous results in Umbria than in other regions.

Gubbio, then, is a small Umbrian town with a population of about 9,000 (a little under 40,000 in the commune), but with public buildings worthy of a national capital, and it was at one time an independent state. Its *Palazzo dei Consoli* is one of the most beautiful and impressive Gothic buildings in Italy, with an immense hall. Its museum contains one exhibit that is unique – the *Tavole Eugubine*, seven bronze tablets that were found near the Roman theatre in 1444 and have fascinated historians ever since. On them are engraved liturgical instructions for the various types of augury, and they date from about 200 B.C., but their chief interest lies in the fact that five of them are in Umbrian, one of the early Italian languages which has not yet been deciphered, but is believed to be almost identical with Etruscan. I have already mentioned the fact that Gubbio was one of the great ceramic towns, and one of its early craftsmen invented a red lustre that aroused bitter jealousy elsewhere. Its pottery, with deceptively naïve flower patterns, still attracts thousands of holiday-makers in search of presents for those at home.

I find the beauty of Gubbio strongly tinged with melancholy, and I am not surprised that it is one of those cities where several of the older houses had, beside and a little above the main entrance, a small door called the *porta del morto* through which nobody passed except in a coffin. But also I have to admit that I may be biased – the first time I went there, it was raining so heavily and so persistently that I never left the car; after sitting in it on the main piazza, peering through misted windows at the Palazzo dei Consoli for upwards of an hour, I drove sadly back to Perugia; the second time I went there, it was so hot that I failed in my intention to climb the steep hill up which the stalwarts carry the *ceri* every year – to the Duomo, where Gubbio's patron saint, St Ubaldo, lies in a glass coffin, and to the Ducal Palace, copied from that of Urbino.

It was to Gubbio that St Francis came, to deal with a wolf that had terrorised the inhabitants. Reproached for its behaviour, (and doubtless amazed to hear a kind word from a human being) the wolf burst into tears, promised never again to frighten anybody, and stretched out its paw to make peace. It subsequently became such a favourite with the people of Gubbio that, when it died, they buried it in holy ground.

Most people go from Gubbio either to Perugia or to Assisi; we made a long détour in order to visit Cortona. We were wise to go there although more sensible people than I would do so on the way between Arezzo and Perugia. Most people on that way, however, do not visit Cortona at all; they race along the main road at the foot of the steep hill on which this ancient Etruscan city stands – so ancient a city that its inhabitants claim it was 'the mother of Troy and the grandmother of Rome'.

It was almost certainly an Umbrian stronghold before the Etruscans took it over in the eighth or seventh century B.C., and its walls in places must be at least 2,500 years old. But in later years it suffered even more than most Tuscan cities in the fratricidal wars, and in 1258, it was so effectively destroyed by troops from its neighbour, Arezzo, that its inhabitants were refugees for three years, after which the Sienese lent them 800 workmen to help them to rebuild their city. Some three miles outside the walls is the church of Santa Maria del Calcinaio, which is one of the most perfect churches of the Renaissance; and the Museo Diocesano has a good collection of pictures, including several by Luca Signorelli, who was born here, and also one of the most beautiful and gentle of Fra Angelico's many 'Annunciations'.

But most visitors to Cortona come there on account of its Etruscan museum in the Palazzo Pretoria, a magnificent thirteenth-century building with a staircase that is breath-taking in both senses of the phrase. For the excellent little museum contains one article that every other Etruscan museum would give a lot to possess – a bronze, circular oil lamp, over 40 centimetres in diameter which, presumably, once hung in an important Etruscan tomb. The centre of this lamp, which has 16 wick-holders, is a Gorgon's head, surrounded by an intricate and very beautiful pattern of wild animals and dolphins, satyrs and sirens, and with a head of Bacchus between each pair of wick-holders. (Sixteen was the number of gods the Etruscans assigned to the 16 regions into which they divided the sky.) This lamp was found in 1840 in a ditch just outside the city, and it must be nearly 2,500 years old. If you have not yet visited any Etruscan tombs, there are several mounds, like the barrows on Salisbury Plain, in the neighbourhood of Cortona – the local people call them 'melons'. The best-known of the few that are open to the public is near the Santa Maria del Calcinaio, miscalled the Tomb of Pythagoras, because somebody confused 'Cortona' with 'Croton' in Southern Italy, where Pythagoras in fact did die.

Brother Elias, who might be called the general director of the Franciscan movement, was born in Cortona and returned there to die in 1253 after he had quarrelled with almost everybody, including his fellow Franciscans, the Emperor and the Pope. He was responsible for the immense Franciscan church in Assisi, so terribly out of keeping with the poverty and simplicity which made St Francis so widely beloved. Presumably, without his initiative, we should not now have the Giotto frescoes, but he became the bitter enemy of Brother Leo, the favourite disciple, secretary and confessor of St Francis during his lifetime and the leader of the so-called Zealots after the saint's death. The quarrel between these two men, each intensely religious and devoted to St Francis, came to a head when Brother Leo broke the marble box which Elias had put outside the church to collect money for its completion. For this, Elias ordered him to be scourged, and this treatment of Francis's dearest disciple so angered other Franciscans that Elias was deposed from his post as Minister General of the Order.

Cortona is now a quiet and austere little city, too small for its ancient walls, which in Etruscan times were more than three kilometres in circumference. Anyone who has the energy to climb its steep streets to the empty land near the sixteenth-century fortress wil have splendid views, westwards across the plain towards Siena and its mountains, southwards down the valley to Lake Trasimene, the scene of Hannibal's great victory over the Romans in 217 B.C. The road to Perugia passes along the narrow strip of land between the hills and the lake, between Borghetto and Passignano, where he trapped and killed some 15,000 Romans. A neighbouring village recalls the bloody event – it is called Sanguinetto. But nowadays the visitors to Borghetto and Passignano are not soldiers, but holiday-makers, attracted by the largest lake of the Italian peninsula.

11. Perugia and Assisi

Perugia stands on a bluff, 1,000 feet above the Tiber and its plain. The road up to it goes a long way to explain the slightly reserved and introspective character of its inhabitants – it is very steep, with many alarming curves and bends which emphasise its remoteness from the rest of the world. Almost every book I have read about Umbria contains some derogatory adjective about this city – even Michael Adams writes that 'Perugia has never come to terms with the twentieth century, but lies there on its hilltop, glowering down the Umbrian plain at its old enemies, malicious and restless and resentful, licking the wounds of history and finding, one suspects, a dark pleasure in the recollections of past enmities.'

And yet, despite a worse reputation for civic disturbance than almost any other city in Italy, even before the end of the thirteenth century it had a university that attracted large numbers of foreign students. And how odd that a fine baroque palace, just outside the Arco Etrusco (part Etruscan, part Roman and part Renaissance) houses the *Università per Stranieri*, which attracts more than 3,000 foreign students a year to the Umbrian capital!

Possibly Perugia's greatest period was when it was one of the twelve towns of the Etruscan league that ruled the western half of Central Italy when Rome was little more than a village. Down on the plain, near the beginning of the long, steep climb to the city, is an Etruscan necropolis, with a large and important 'tomb of the Volumnii', dating from the second half of the second century B.C., with nine small rooms opening into a central place, rather after the pattern of a Roman house of that time. As in Tarquinia, but in too few other necropolises, the contents of the tomb have been left where they were, or have been removed to a small museum above it.

Travellers who have no opportunity of visiting Tarquinia or Chiusi should not miss this tomb and the Etruscan collection in the Musei Civici, housed in an old Dominican convent. The museum has an exceptionally good collection of urns, coins and bronzes, as well as a tablet on which is one of the longest Etruscan inscriptions yet discovered – about 100 words. Pottering about in the steep streets of the mediaeval quarter, one frequently comes across lengths of the Etruscan fortifications.

By the time the last of the Volumnii had been brought to this tomb, the power of the Romans was spreading. They captured Perugia in 40 B.C. and turned it into a *municipium*. But it knew no durable peace. In the struggle for power after the murder of Julius Caesar, it was reduced to ashes by the troops of his great-nephew, Octavianus (who had given himself the title of Augustus). He proceeded to rebuild the town and called it Augusta Perusia, and the Arco Etrusca, mentioned above, is also known as the Arco d'Augusto, to record his interest in rebuilding the city.

The Dark Ages – roughly the period of seven centuries following upon the fall of the Roman Empire in 475 – were even darker for Perugia than for many other cities. But the people were tough, and it must have been during that period that they developed their rather cynical sense of humour. No incident in their history could be more typical of their toughness than their resistance to the great leader of the Goths, Totila, in the sixth century. He had besieged the city for seven years, at the end of which the defenders were so close to starvation that many of them wanted to surrender. Not, however, their bishop, Ercolano. At his orders, they fed their last ox on wheat, and threw its fattened carcase over the city walls so that the Goths, who were themselves very hungry, would not realise the degree of hunger within the gates. Unfortunately, this attempt to discourage the enemy was a failure, for a young priest, either ignorant of the ruse or a spy, shouted details of the starvation inside the walls to a Goth soldier outside. Surrender became inevitable, and Ercolano was executed on the piazza that now bears his name. He became the city's patron saint. In the words of a Perugian of many generations, he deserved this honour for three reasons – he was *perugino, furbo ed un santo* – Perugian, artful and a saint.

When nobody was besieging Perugia, the Perugians still had little peace. No other ruling family in Italy had a worse reputation for murderous brutality, mixed with *panache* and a considerable respect for the arts, than the Baglioni, who decided the destinies of the city from the end of the fourteenth century until 1540, when Pope Paul III sent an army to avenge the murder of a Papal Legate by destroying the Baglioni palaces and erecting, on the half-ruined houses, an immense fortress known as the Rocca Paolina. Above one of the gateways of the fortress were carved the words – *Ad coercendam Perusinorum audaciam* – 'For the repression of Perugian audacity.'

To my mind, this Rocca Paolina is the most fascinating sight in Perugia. The Pope was in a hurry to have it built, and the architect in charge, none other than Sangallo the Younger, who has so many of Italy's most elegant buildings to his credit, wasted no time in razing the whole area of Baglioni dwellings to the ground. Where possible, he incorporated their walls and built over the top of them, so that the present Palazzo del Governo now stands above not only the fortress (which the Perugians did their utmost to destroy after they had thrown off the control of the popes in 1860) but also the remains of a cobbled street and the houses that flanked it. Sangallo being an artist as well as an architect, here and there one sees a piece of mediaeval decoration, an elegant doorway or window, that one would scarcely expect to see inside a massive fortress.

The result is both fantastic and beautiful. Some great pillars soar upwards into the darkness to form arches that support the present surface of the outside world. Other arches are superimposed on the still older columns of a Baglioni mansion. Still other arches are those that led into these mansions. And very clever lighting converts this cemetery of stone into a place of bewildering beauty. Piranesi, one imagines, would have been ecstatic.

When the Baglioni had obliterated their principal rivals, the Oddi, they turned against each other. In the year 1500, one of the last of them, Grifonetto, who had married into the famous Sforza family, took advantage of the fact that the whole family had collected to celebrate the wedding of one of his cousins to a member of the even more famous Colonna family to have them all murdered. Only one, Gianpaolo, escaped. Grifonetto was soon murdered, outside the church of Sant' Ercolano, by members of Gianpaolo's bodyguard, and Gianpaolo then avenged his family by ordering the execution of more than 100 alleged conspirators. Their heads were then impaled on stakes fixed into the side of the Palazzo dei Priori, and a fresco on a neighbouring wall pictured the leaders hanging upside down by one leg – a favourite form of execution in Italy at the time. Gianpaolo was later murdered in the Castel Sant' Angelo in Rome, at the behest of Pope Leo X, and of his two sons one murdered a son of Grifonetto and was himself killed while fighting in Southern Italy, and the other, promoted to be leader of the Florentine army, betrayed the city to the Pope, against whose forces he was pledged to defend it. It was his son, Ridolfo – the last member of the family – who ordered the murder of the Papal Legate in 1540.

And yet the city was a mass of contradictions. The Perugians were too busily engaged in wars of one kind or another to find money to finish their cathedral (and the Baglioni once used the unfinished building as a fortress) but they appear to have played a great part in the development of one of the most startling moods of religious hysteria that swept across Europe in the Middle Ages. Flagellation, as an act of discipline or penance, has been known at many periods and in many religions, but the *Battuti*, the flagellant brotherhood started by a Perugian monk called Ranieri, was adopted with fanaticism by the inhabitants and spread through Central Europe as far east as Poland and as far north as the Netherlands. The *Battuti* flogged themselves with thongs fitted with four iron points, and their brotherhood created such widespread disturbances that many cities shut their gates against them and, in 1349, Pope Clement VI found it necessary to condemn them as heretics whereafter the Inquisition put the more fervent of these strange Christians to death.

In the intervals between their battles, the Perugians used to listen deeply moved, to a preacher who addressed them from the charming little pulpit outside the northern flank of the Duomo. This remarkable man was San Bernardino da Siena – actually he was born at Massa Marittima, farther south, but he was brought to Siena as a small boy. In both Siena and Perugia his influence was immense. He called upon his congregation to make bonfires of their luxuries, their fine clothes, their mirrors and all other vanities. He set a good example – like St Francis, he came of a wealthy family, but he lived in such poverty and went around in such rags that the Sienese threw stones at him. His poverty, of course, gave additional weight to his appeals for reform, and he had the same hypnotic effect on his congregations as Savonarola was to have on the Florentines a century later, although he used colloquial down-to-earth language such as very few saints can ever have used. He would have been a splendid revivalist preacher were it not that few revivalists have a strong sense of humour. The Perugians burned their baubles, they listened with tears in their eyes to his condemnation of violence – and, within a few days or a few weeks, there would again be murder, vendettas, fighting. It is a little strange that this man, in some ways so severe, is commemorated by the most elegant building in Perugia – the Oratorio di San Bernardino, the façade of which was the work of a Florentine sculptor, Agostino d'Antonio di Duccio, who did most of the plastic decoration of the Malatestiano temple in Rimini. The façade of the Oratorio in Perugia makes use of both coloured marble and terracotta. Many of the marble figures, like those of the Maitani bas-reliefs on the façade of Orvieto cathedral, have taken on the patina of old ivory.

Even during the bloodiest disturbances, Perugia's artists were painting the serene and gentle pictures which were characteristic of the Umbrian school. The most famous and prolific of them was Pietro Vannucci better known as Il Perugino, who taught Raphael when he was in his early twenties and whose sentimentality possibly did the young man as much harm as good. (It was only after he had moved to Florence that Raphael developed, with astonishing rapidity, into a great artist.) Personally, I find the backgrounds of Perugino's pictures more interesting than his simple and gentle Madonnas.

Perugia's main street runs along the crest of the hill. It is called the Corso Vannucci, in honour of Perugino and it leads into the Piazza 4 Novembre, which is certainly one of the most beautiful squares in Italy. This beauty does not derive from the Cathedral, as it does in so many Italian cities. Its façade has never been completed although the marble for this purpose was once bought, but was used elsewhere. The beauty of the piazza is due to the façade of the Palazzo Pubblico opposite and to the fountain in the middle of the square.

Italian architects have always been exceptionally clever with fountains and flights of steps. The fountain at Perugia, built in 1277 by Fra Bevignate, has few rivals. The panels round one of the two marble basins, portraying in relief scenes out of Aesop's Fables as well as Old Testament subjects, were carved by Niccolà and Giovanni Pisano, the creators of the pulpits in the Pisan Baptistery and the Cathedral respectively. The fountain is signed by both father and son and is dated 1278, which means that it was Niccolà's last important work. His contribution to the fountain is believed to be the carving round the lower and larger of the basins.

On the east side of the piazza is the episcopal palace, where five popes were elected. A strange love-hate relationship seems to have existed between the popes and the Perugians. One of four popes who died in Perugia was Innocent III, under whose rule the Papacy achieved more temporal power than at any other time. Another was Martin IV, who excommunicated the city, to which the people replied by burning his effigy on the piazza. He made up his quarrel, came to Perugia, and died there after eating too many eels. The other two popes were Urban IV, who is believed to have been poisoned, and Benedict XI, who was very fond of figs and was insufficiently suspicious when offered a dish of them by a nun who, it is generally believed, was in the pay of the King of France. The episcopal palace, according to one historian, had so much wine in its cellars that on one occasion it was used to extinguish a fire in the nearby Palazzo dei Priori.

Of the popes elected in Perugia, none was more strange than Celestino V, who managed to abdicate after a bare five months. After the death of Nicholas IV, rivalry between European rulers and fighting in Rome between the two dominant families, the Orsini and the Colonna, had prevented the choice of a new pope for two years and three months. In 1292, during a conclave in Perugia, somebody suggested an almost unknown hermit, Pietro di Morrone, who lived in a cave in the Abruzzi mountains. In so far as he was known, his reputation was one of complete saintliness, and the cardinals recognised the importance of choosing a man devoid of worldly ambitions. When told of his election, the hermit – 80 years of age – tried to run away, but he was taken almost by force to Aquila where he was crowned Pope, and then to Rome, where he is supposed to have lived in an artificial cave in his palace. Too simple and honest to understand papal politics, he fell entirely under the influence of Charles II, King of Naples, to the great distress of

many cardinals, who finally set a new precedent by allowing
him to resign. His successor took him into what is called nowadays 'protective custody' and he died, saintly but bewildered,
18 months later.

Across the square from the Duomo is the Palazzo dei Priori,
or Palazzo Pubblico, with a very beautiful outside staircase. The
Palazzo is an immense building, which houses not only the
municipal offices and the city archives but also the *pinacoteca*,
the Umbrian national art gallery. One room in it is of particular interest to Englishmen. It is called the *Sala del Mal-
consiglio*, the Bad Advice having been in favour of releasing
some mercenaries who had been captured in a battle against
the English condottiere, Sir John Hawkwood. These prisoners
drafted an appeal in which they called themselves 'your English vassals'. This probably flattered the priors, and they re-
leased the men; in the following year, Hawkwood again fought
the Perugians, killed several thousands of them and captured
the German condottiere in command of their force. The Sala
dei Priori is grandiose, and in another room, the Sala Rossa, a
painting of Pope Julius III restoring the city rights shows the
splendour with which the councillors decked themselves out
on great occasions.

The upper floor houses the *pinacoteca*, containing mainly
Umbrian works, some of which suggest that beauty is not always truth – there is about them a kind of gentle escapism
which was, I suppose, an unconscious reaction against the
brutality by which the artists were surrounded. And, for that
same reason, they were tremendously popular in their day. But
the collection is a very fine one : it is also unusually charming
on account of the rural backgrounds of so many of the pictures.
Indeed, this development of interest in depth and background
in order to emphasise the principal figures was probably Umbria's most important contribution to painting. Pinturicchio and
Perugino, his teacher, are, of course, well represented in the
gallery although Perugino did even better work in his frescoes in
the Collegio del Cambio, adjoining the Palazzo dei Priori.

This Collegio was the chamber of commerce and the office of money-changers in the fifteenth century, and Perugino and his assistants spent eight years on its frescoes. It is quite probable, but unproven, that Raphael was one of these assistants and that he painted on these walls even before, at the age of 22, he painted his first known work in the disused church of San Severo. The small Audience Hall in the Collegio del Cambio contains some very remarkable carving and intarsio work which should not be overlooked in the attempt to identify the rather confusing subjects of the frescoes. Daniel is said by some to be a portrait of Raphael and Jeremiah of Pinturicchio. On a column between two arches on the left side there is a portrait of Perugino himself – 'a tough-looking, ugly little man', writes H. V. Morton, 'with a thin mouth and eyes which are calculating and at the same time apprehensive.... Though it may not be a kind face, it is a pathetic one'. Personally, I find this judgment rather too severe. In any case, there must have been other qualities besides great ability as an artist to have brought him from extreme poverty in his youth to international fame in middle age. And it is worth recording that, in order to paint these frescoes in the city of his adoption, he refused the very tempting invitation to decorate the Cappella di San Brizio in the Orvieto cathedral (which, in the event, was so brilliantly decorated by Luca Signorelli).

Visitors are unlikely to see one of the strangest and most prized possessions of Perugia, for it is on display only five times a year. In one of the chapels in the Duomo is a casket inside 14 other caskets, the keys of which are entrusted each to a different official. The innermost casket contains one of the most unexpected of all holy records – the wedding ring of the Madonna. Adam of Usk, the first British pilgrim known to have crossed the St Gotthard Pass at the beginning of the fifteenth century, noted among the sacred relics in St John Lateran in Rome 'the altar St John had in the desert ... the table on which our Lord Jesus Christ supped with his disciples; also the rod of Moses and Aaron; also a shoulder blade of St Lawrence; also the sheet in which Christ was rolled on the cross' and several other interesting but slightly improbable relics. But in those days people were much more credulous than they are today. Barbarian invaders of Italy were often more interested in looting bones than money, since they could sell them with such profit to believers at home. I find it a little surprising that the Madonna's wedding ring should be so venerated in this age of scepticism. The ring was brought to Perugia in 1472 by a monk who had 'piously' stolen it from the Franciscans at Chiusi.

It would, of course, be absurd to go to Perugia without also going to Assisi which, to very many Catholics, is second only to Rome in holiness. For that very reason, I find it a difficult subject to write about. St Francis was born in Assisi, where his name has been commercialised as much as has that of Jesus in Nazareth and the Holy Sepulchre in Jerusalem. I have so deep a dislike of this cheapening of religion that, were it not for the artists who came to Assisi to commemorate the deeds of this extraordinary man in their frescoes, I should have been tempted to avoid the town altogether, with the excuse that I had already written about its greatest citizen in an earlier chapter. His experiences in the monastery of La Verna, I could have argued, were probably as important to him – since it was there that he received the stigmata – as his foundation of the Franciscan Order in Assisi.

Had I dismissed Assisi in a paragraph or two, on the strength of one very short visit there several years ago, I should have been guilty of a lamentable dereliction of duty and error of judgment. I found on my return visit that the personality of '*Il Poverello*' is more powerful than the pomp which goes so far towards concealing it.

Few things about St Francis are more fascinating than the speed with which his ideas were accepted. He was born in 1182 and was only 26 when he founded the Franciscan Order. He gained the Pope's approval of it within two years. A mere 14 years later, in 1224, he received the stigmata in the monas-

tery of La Verna, and two years later he died. In this short
life, his influence was such that Franciscan monasteries were
founded in many parts of Europe. Two years after his death,
Pope Gregory IX canonized him and laid the foundation-stone of
the Franciscan church at Assisi.

St Francis had somehow found time to travel in many
countries, and even went to Egypt while the Crusaders were besieging Damietta, a very important city in the delta of the Nile.
He was taken prisoner, but managed to be brought before the
Sultan in the hope that peace might be made between Christians
and Muslims, presumably by the conversion of the Muslims to
Christianity. In this, not surprisingly, he failed, but it says much
for both men that the Sultan treated him with great courtesy
and sent him back, a free man, to the Crusaders' camp. Sir
Stephen Runciman's version of this incident is probably the
correct one – the Sultan decided that 'anyone so simple, so
gentle and so dirty must be mad', and he accorded him the
respect due to 'a man who has been touched by God' (*A History of the Crusades*, Cambridge University Press, 1951).

St Francis died just outside the Porziuncola, a small and
simple chapel five kilometres out of Assisi and hidden inside
the walls of a large sixteenth-century basilica, Santa Maria degli
Angeli, the mother church of the Franciscan Order. *Porziuncola*
means 'a small portion' of ground, a little clearing in the woods
that the Benedictines from the abbey on the higher slopes of
Monte Subasio gave to Francis as the headquarters for his
newly-founded order. The chapel in this clearing was already
very old, but had been repaired by St Benedict in the sixth century. He is said to have been responsible for the two large
entrance arches, unsuitable for the very tiny chapel to which
they give access; he had them built because, while praying in
the chapel, he had a vision of huge crowds of worshippers
arriving there – as, indeed, they do for the Pardon of St Francis,
on the anniversary of his death on 4 October. At his request,
Francis was brought to the Porziuncola to die on the naked

earth, where there is now a chapel called the Cappella del Transito.

But in Santa Maria degli Angeli, as also in the great Franciscan church where he is buried, it is difficult to envisage the utter humility and simplicity of the little man in whose honour they were built. Fortunately, the convent of San Damiano is only two and a half kilometres outside the town and it has no huge church to record the fact that St Francis here formed the sister Order of the Poor Clares. St Clare had belonged to a wealthy family but, inspired by the example of St Francis, gave up all material belongings to retire to this disused church which the Benedictines also handed over to St Francis. It was for forty years the home of the Poor Clares – they then moved to the existing convent in Assisi – and it is so poor, so primitive, that here one can begin to appreciate the sincerity and holiness of the earliest Franciscans. St Francis is said to have written his famous song of praise and thanksgiving, the Canticle of the Sun, in the garden of this convent.

Most visitors to Assisi, of course, are less interested in the lives of the earliest Franciscans than in the works of art which St Francis inspired. They are in such a hurry to visit the two churches, one above the other, of San Francesco that some of them never go to the centre of Assisi at all, although the Piazza del Comune, site of the one-time Roman forum, has not only very attractive mediaeval buildings, but also a remarkably fine Roman Temple of Minerva (now a Christian church) with its portico of six magnificent Corinthian columns, squeezed alongside the mediaeval Torre del Popolo – two admirable but very different examples of Italian architecture.

The lower church was the scene of one of those unedifying mediaeval incidents which concerned the body of St Francis but which go some way to explain the wild-fire success of his doctrine of simplicity and poverty. I have already mentioned that invading troops who sacked Rome sometimes preferred bones to gold – they were less conspicuous and could be sold at a great profit to Christians north of the Alps. There was also, of course, a strong and genuine religious feeling which gave these relics their financial value. Probably for both these reasons, Perugians were very anxious to capture the bones of St Francis, and Brother Elias who had taken over the management of the Franciscan Order, was running no risks. Two years after the Pope had laid the foundation stone of the lower church St Francis was buried in it. But exactly where only Brother Elias and, presumably, a few workmen knew – as soon as the coffin had been brought into the church the doors were locked against the would-be congregation – including an indignant papal legate – and it was put into a prepared tomb cut into the rock. It was so well concealed, in fact, from Perugians or any others who might want to steal it that it was not found until the Franciscans, early in the nineteenth century, were given permission by the pope to make a search for it. After two months of tunnelling from beneath the altar, they found the coffin under slabs of travertine marble. Amongst the dust of St Francis's bones, they found some coins that had been put into the coffin, (including some from Lucca, dated 1181 and 1208). In the dark crypt in the centre of which now stands the saint's tomb are buried four of his original disciples, including Brother Leo who was his closest friend and confessor. Brother Elias, who was mainly responsible for hiding the saint's coffin and for building the two churches above it, is not one of the remaining three. One cannot help thinking that St Francis would have approved of this exclusion, since he would so have disapproved of the pomp and circumstance which Elias decided were necessary if the Order was to grow, but Brother Elias also deserves our gratitude, since he was mainly responsible for bringing so many artists to Assisi.

It is not always realised that St Francis was unwittingly one of the prophets of the Renaissance. His contemporary, Emperor Frederick II, in southern Italy, had so openly broken away from long-accepted conventions and beliefs that the popes excommunicated him. New ideas were reaching Europe through Sicily and southern Spain. But most artists showed a marked reluctance to portray the Madonna, the infant Christ, the apostles as ordinary human beings. They had human shape but the popes or priests who commissioned the pictures would probably have been shocked had their humanity overshadowed their godliness. Roughly another two centuries were to elapse before the demand for reality in painting encouraged artists to use their own wives or mistresses as models for the Virgin Mary.

But here was Francis, *Il Poverello*, finding godliness among lepers and unwashed beggars. In every Italian church at Christmas-time, there is a *presepio*, with little figures to represent Mary, the infant Christ, the farm animals in the stable in Bethlehem. St Francis obtained the pope's permission to put the first *presepio* in a village church. This realistic attempt to show the humblest onlooker the humble conditions of Christ's birth was revolutionary; it aroused the artist's interest in the life and scenery outside his own home. Here was an escape from the rigid representation of the Holy Family.

Cimabue's portrait of St Francis in the lower church must surely be one of the first naturalistic portraits? Giotto, one of Cimabue's pupils, was born about 40 years after the death of St Francis, and his cycle of frescoes of the life of the saint, in the upper church, portray a very different man from the Francis portrayed by Cimabue, but they have immense sincerity, strength and sense of perspective. Experts differ greatly about the merits of one painter and the demerits of another; they seem all to agree that Giotto was the first 'modern' painter.

12. Umbria South of Perugai

In an earlier chapter, dealing with the narrow strip of land between the mountains and the Adriatic, I advised readers to limit their explorations of the Apennines to their western slopes or, for purposes of this book, to Umbria. Perugia is a little to the north of centre. South of this city lies some of the most beautiful country I know.

Perhaps the pleasantest way to approach it is to leave the *autostrada* at Orvieto, which is near the south-western border of Umbria, and to take the mountain road to Todi. Central Italy is not normally a good region for picnics – the hillsides are too steep and the plains are too densely cultivated to provide such pleasant spots as one finds almost anywhere on the great plateau of Central France. But the Orvieto – Todi road is a glorious exception. Along its 42 kilometres there is only one small town, Prodo (a village promoted to the status of a town by a fine castle), and there are dozens of spots from which one enjoys a tremendous view of the mountains away to the south. And Todi seen from the west – a small town standing proudly on the summit of a high hill – is very impressive.

It is exceptional in that it has three sets of walls in unusually good condition – Etruscan, Roman and Mediaeval. Parts of the Etruscan wall, with stones laid in horizontal courses, one course being broad and the next narrow, are of particular interest to Etruscologists. Todi was called Tuder in Roman and Etruscan days, and must have been an important town, although it was a few miles away from the Via Flaminia. As well as its walls, it has the ruins of a large building believed to have been a temple of Mars. According to some experts, the Etruscans found Tuder already a flourishing city and never managed to capture it. The Romans did capture it but added 'of Mars' to its name in recognition of its help during the Punic wars. It defied both Totila in the sixth century and Frederick II in the thirteenth. It is now, like Cortona, Volterra and many other ancient cities, much smaller than its walls; it has come down in the world.

Outside the walls there is one of the purest Renaissance churches in Umbria, Santa Maria della Consolazione, in the shape of a Greek cross. The centre and each of the four arms of the cross are covered by domes, and the general effect is unusual in this Umbrian landscape of olives and cypresses. In common with Sangallo's church of San Biagio, just outside Montepulciano, its architect would seem to have been strongly influenced by the work of Bramante, and some writers claim that, on a small scale, it is as Bramante would have wished St Peter's in Rome to be.

I find Todi much more beautiful than the normal photographs of it would lead one to expect, for the most usual picture is of the square, unfinished façade of the cathedral, with a flat roof and, on one side, a square tower. True, the rose window and the central doorway, flanked by two similar but much smaller doors, are attractive, and so is the magnificent, broad flight of steps leading up to it. But the view of the piazza from the Duomo is far more attractive than the view of the Duomo from the piazza, for the Palazzo del Popolo, the Palazzo dei Priori and the Palazzo del Capitano at the far end of it are solid, severe, self-confident, but very beautiful. All three date from the thirteenth century. It is increasingly difficult to find adjectives that adequately express the pleasure given by the main square in so many small Italian towns; all I say of the piazza at Todi (the great flagstones of which apparently cover the vaults of an old Roman cistern) is that it ranks with those of Siena, San Gimignano, Ravenna, Massa Marittima, Pienza and Viterbo.

Even farm houses in the Middle Ages often had crenellated towers – towers the tops of which have square gaps through which the defenders could fire at the enemy. These cut-out portions are called 'crenels' and the solid portions between them are 'merlons'. The tops of merlons built when the Guelfs were in power were horizontal whereas those built by the Ghibellines were fish-tailed, and sometimes one comes across a Guelf building to which Ghibelline merlons have obviously been added, or *vice versa*. In the case of these two important buildings in Todi, the Palazzo del Popolo displays its loyalty to the Guelfs, whereas the Palazzo del Capitano is Ghibelline – its fish-tails look as though they had been added in a hurry. This latter palazzo, which has a fine exterior staircase, also has great arches which open the ground floor to the street on three sides – it is, in fact, an architectural predecessor to the modern office buildings on stilts, which sacrifice the ground floor in order to provide parking room for the tenants' cars. Not much new under the sun!

Near the fortress at the top of the town, there is the church of St Fortunato, with a very fine portal and, since it was being built from 1292 to 1460, an interesting mixture of Gothic and Renaissance. It has a fresco by that rare artist, Masolino, best known for his frescoes in collaboration with Masaccio, in the Brancoli Chapel of Santa Maria del Carmine in Florence. In the crypt is the tomb of the Franciscan poet, Fra Jacopone, the author of the thirteenth century Latin hymn, *Stabat Mater*, which has been set to music by many different composers, including Palestrina, Pergolesi, Stanford, Rossini and Verdi. He had been a rich and cynical lawyer until his wife was killed by falling masonry while they were dancing at a wedding. Only then did he discover that, under her fine clothes, she was wearing a hair-shirt, the symbol of penitence. This evidence of her inner and religious life, of which he had known nothing, so moved him that he became one of the strictest followers of St Francis, one of the severest critics of papal luxury, and the author of devotional poetry.

*   *   *

Misled by a guidebook in which I normally place great confidence, we decided to visit Giano dell'Umbria, alleged to be a very small, fortified town, crowned by two castles. It stands on a hill not far from the road between Todi and Montefalco. We reached it by way of a village with the unusual name of Bastardo, and there seemed to me to be little else that was unusual. Instead of two romantic and ancient castles. I found one modern-looking building with crenellations such as one sees decorating the roofs of phoney castles along the Riviera. This disappointment, coupled with the fact that it began to rain, undoubtedly affected my judgment of my next destination, Montefalco, so often referred to as 'the balcony of Umbria'.

From the 'balcony' we could see nothing but grey cloud, instead of the peaceful valley of the Clitunno. The Palazzo Comunale dates from 1270, but has been renovated, and the stucco that defaces it calls for removal or repair. The town was sacked by Frederick II – an emperor for whom my admiration diminishes as I find out how many little towns his troops destroyed – and has suffered many other misfortunes in the course of its long history. But, according to Michael Adams, it still manages to preserve 'a special Franciscan character, a mildness of temperament, which earned it the title of "a strip of heaven fallen to earth", and which encouraged the growth of an artistic tradition, gentle and unsophisticated, which can claim its share in the later achievements of the Umbrian painters of the Renaissance'.

However extensive the views from Montefalco may be on a fine day, its principal glory is its collection of paintings in the former church of San Francesco. The church door has three locks, and a woman with three large and antiquated keys had great difficulty in opening it for us. One soon realised the reasons for these precautions – here is one of the finest collections of Umbrian paintings in existence. Most people come to see the Benozzo Gozzoli frescoes of the life of St Francis and other subjects. They are wise to do so, for the colours are marvellously preserved. St Francis preaching to the birds is particularly endearing and the painting of the devils being driven from Arezzo contains many of those architectural details that so delight students of the Middle Ages. The walled town in the valley below St Francis and his avian congregation is Bevagna which, under the name of Mevania, was an important station on the Roman Via Flaminia. Among the other artists represented in this church are Perugino, Melozzo da Forlì, F. Melanzio, Lo Spagna, Ottaviano Nelli and Nicolò da Foligno – Umbrian painters who, like Umbria itself, are less well-known than they merit.

As one drives down from this 'balcony of Umbria' to the valley of the Clitunno, one sees a white triangle on the opposite slope of the Apennines–Trevi, as different as it could be from the fountain in Rome to which it has given its name. Here there are no tourists, seeking the local fountain so that they can throw their coins into it. As they travel from Perugia to Rome they see this white town climbing the steep slope, but very few of them go up to it. The guidebooks neglect it, for it cannot boast much about artistic or architectural treasures, apart from a signed fresco by Perugino and several pictures by Lo Spagna, a pupil of Perugino, who was very faithful to this part of Umbria. Below the town is an elegant early Renaissance church, the Madonna delle Lacrime, which contains most of these works. Probably it is because of this neglect by the guidebooks that Trevi has more of the atmosphere of the Middle Ages than almost any other Umbrian town. Like several other hill towns in the region, it has streets paved with cobbles or old bricks, and one attractive feature is the variety of neat little patterns in cobble stones in front of each patrician house.

Most people on their way to Spoleto and the south would be driving along the road from Perugia. They should not fail to visit Spello – *Colonia Julia Hispellum* – which was a very important place in Roman times. One enters it through a fine Roman gate called the Porta Venere surmounted by three figures, the middle one, presumably, being Venus herself. The narrow streets, mostly paved with old brick, wind uphill to the ruins of a castle, from which you have a wide view of the valley – too wide a view in my opinion, and dotted with so many modern and ugly buildings that I should not climb up there a second time. One of the attractions of the place – as also of Trevi, Assisi and other neighbouring towns – is the use in many of the buildings of a lovely rose-pink stone from Monte Subasio, the great hill on which they stand. But the principal attraction of Spello is the church of Santa Maria Maggiore, where the Baglioni Chapel (named after the ruthless rulers of Perugia) contains some of the best frescoes ever painted by Pinturicchio.

At the side of the main road between Trevi and Spoleto is the *Fonti del Clitunno*. One comes first to a notice referring to a little temple, the back of which is visible from the road. This 'tempietta' is now the disused church of San Salvatore, which was one of the very early churches built after Emperor Constantine had become a Christian and had thus removed the fear of religious persecution. It contains a fresco which is said to be the oldest fresco in Umbria, dating from the seventh century. At one time it was believed to be the temple described by Pliny as having been ancient even in his day, but this claim is no longer made, although some of its marble has damaged Roman inscriptions which might have come from the original temple.

Two kilometres nearer Spoleto, and much better marked to catch the attention of the passing motorist, is the reach of water praised by Pliny the younger, by Virgil in the *Georgics* and by many later poets, including Carducci, Dryden and Byron. This is the *Fonti di Clitunno*. The 'Clitumnus' was personified as a god by the Romans; it was visited by at least two Roman emperors – Honorius and Caligula, who came there with all his court. The festival of the god Clitumnus, which lasted from 21 April to 1 May, brought spectators from as far away as Rome.

The *Fonti*'s popularity is even more deserved today, when traffic is so much noisier, heavier and more harassing. The road is only a few yards away, and yet the poplars and the weeping willows, the gentle flow of the limpid water, and the extraordinary variety of water plants – I refuse to call them weeds – combine to induce such a feeling of peace that one ceases to notice the passing traffic. This place is not so very strange to English eyes – I know reaches of the Test and the Itchen which are very similar. But I have seen nothing in the least like it anywhere else in Italy, where streams either splash from rock to rock down a hillside or wind their muddy way to the sea. I am sorry to write this, since I love Italy, but the *Fonti di Clitunno* is the only Italian stretch of water I have seen, except on some private estate, that was not cluttered up with old tins, buckets, bedsteads and the like. The water at Clitunno is as clear as God must have intended water to be, and that is almost a miracle.

In fact, the Clitunno has something that even the Test has not got – the water is as smooth as silk, and yet sparkling and alive. There must be scores of small springs in the river bed, each sending to the surface bubbles so small that they do not disturb its smoothness. A surface of watered silk. Small wonder that the Romans believed the white, wide-horned oxen they so admired – and the visitor to Italy can still admire them to-day – were made whiter by the waters of Clitunno.

The best centre for visits to any of these little towns in south-eastern Umbria is, without any doubt, Spoleto. In 1958, Gian Carlo Menotti organised the first Festival of Two Worlds there, and one result is that, except during the festival itself in June and July, there is an unusually wide choice of hotel accommodation for so small a city. But also Spoleto is very attractive, with an immensely long history. The earliest walls were about two kilometres in circumference, and part of those lengths that still remain consists of immense, polygonal and rough-hewn blocks of stone which were probably put there in the sixth century B.C. The Romans made Spoleto a colony in 240 B.C. Twenty-five years later, the Spoletans repelled an attack by

Hannibal, fresh from his great victory over the Romans at Lake Trasimene. According to some writers, this Spoletan resistance gave the Romans the time in which to reorganise their defences; according to others, Hannibal had decided to mop up Roman garrisons all over the country before, with the help of expected reinforcements, he attacked Rome. Naturally enough, the people of Spoleto prefer the former version, and one of the city gates was called the *Porta della Fuga* (the Gate of the Flight) to commemorate Hannibal's failure. The first Bishop of Spoleto, St Brizius, was a contemporary of St Peter.

Nearly eight centuries after Hannibal, the formidable Totila besieged Spoleto but failed to capture it. After the Ostrogoths, the Lombards, or *Longobardi* (Long Beards), crossed the Alps and invaded Italy, which, in theory, was still governed by the Eastern, or Byzantine, Emperor, with headquarters in Constantinople and a western capital in Ravenna. (The complete break between east and west, and the establishment of the Holy Roman Empire came only two centuries later.) The Lombards drove the Byzantine troops down into the 'heel' and 'toe' of Italy and, in order to keep them there, established independent Duchies of Spoleto and Benevento. This meant that Spoleto governed a state which included Assisi in the north and Sulmona in the south, and maintained some degree of independence for more than six centuries, at the end of which it became a part of the Papal States.

Spoleto is on a steep hill, at the top of which is a large castle, the *Rocca*. Lucrezia Borgia lived there in 1499 as papal governor on behalf of her father, Pope Alexander VI; it is now a prison. Unlike most Italian towns, Spoleto has no central square – the busy Piazza del Mercato was once the Roman forum, but it is small and unpretentious. The Piazza della Libertà is more imposing, but one side of it is given up to a wall through the arches of which you look down – as though it were the most ordinary sight in the world – on a Roman theatre. And this is typical of the town – you are constantly confronted by buildings of vastly different periods. There is a (disused) Roman bridge near the northern entrance to the town. There is a Roman amphitheatre. Adjoining the eighteenth-century Palazzo Comunale are interesting ruins of a Roman villa which is said to have belonged to the mother of Emperor Vespasian. A Roman arch has mediaeval rooms built on top of it.

The more important streets run almost parallel to each other along the side of the hill, with steep lanes or flights of steps linking the one to the other at right angles. It should therefore be an easy town in which to find one's way. But there are enough exceptions – since the main roads naturally follow the curving contour lines – to make this rule an unwise one to adopt. The safest procedure is to go steadily uphill, preferably under the arches of the Via di Visiale or up the narrow Vicolo della Basilica – both very picturesque – until you discover the Duomo.

On the way there, you will probably pass the Archbishop's Palace. That would be a mistake – you should go inside its courtyard, in order to visit the twelfth century church of Sant' Eufemia. Its severely simple façade and sturdy interior columns give it the kind of dignity of which, I imagine, St Francis, who often came to Spoleto, must have approved. There is a fantastic contrast between this Romanesque church and, for example, the splendidly flamboyant Baroque of San Filippo Neri a little way down the hill.

Just beyond the Archbishop's Palace, you come to the Duomo which, on account as much of its position as of its architecture (for the façade belongs to several different periods) is one of the most impressive buildings in Umbria. I have referred elsewhere to the magnificent flights of steps that lead up to so many Italian churches – in Todi, for example, and in Massa Marittima. Here, on the contrary, you go down a long staircase, each step of which is so wide that you take three paces to cross it and so shallow that the approach is called a street, and not a staircase.

This cathedral dates from the year after William the Conqueror landed in Britain. Its tower, built partly with blocks of Roman masonry, dates from the twelfth century, and the mosaic of the façade dates from the thirteenth. The lovely Renaissance portico was added nearly three centuries later. On either side of this portico is a small outside pulpit. The staircase‐street down to the piazza in front of the Duomo is called the Via dell' Arringo, a corruption of 'arengo', a meeting place. I conclude that the people were harangued from one or other of these pulpits – or from both pulpits simultaneously, as in Speakers Corner in London's Hyde Park?

This square was the scene in 1155 of one of Spoleto's greatest tragedies. Frederick Barbarossa was on his way back to Germany from Rome, where he had been crowned emperor by Hadrian IV, the only English pope. Barbarossa demanded tribute from Spoleto, as from other cities he passed on his way, but the Spoletans either refused or paid with counterfeit coins. As I have told elsewhere in this book, in order to get himself crowned emperor, he had been compelled to humiliate himself at Viterbo by holding the pope's stirrup while he dismounted, and he must have been in no friendly frame of mind. Indeed, he was so angered by Spoleto's behaviour that he personally led the attack against the city. (The street up which he fought his way near the Roman amphitheatre is still called the Via dell' Assalto.) The Spoletans' last stand was in this piazza in front of the Cathedral. For two days, Barbarossa's army sacked and burnt the town, while those inhabitants who could escape took refuge on Monteluco, the mountain east of Spoleto, which is now the favourite objective for Sunday excursionists.

The frescoes in the choir were painted by Fra Filippo Lippi. He died in Spoleto in 1469, before they were finished and they were completed by his friend, Fra Diamante. Lorenzo the Magnificent had always befriended Filippo and he wanted him to be buried in Florence, where he had spent so much of his life, but the Spoletans refused to give up the body. So Lorenzo commissioned the son, Filippino Lippi, to erect a tomb for his father in Spoleto Cathedral. It includes a medallion of Filippo in the garb of a monk, which he had ceased to be after Lucrezia Buti, a beautiful nun who had been his model for the Virgin Mary in Prato, had produced a son, Filippino. Filippo's adventures which, according to Vasari, had included a period as a slave of the Barbary pirates in North Africa, had landed him in troubles throughout his life, and his death in Spoleto at the age of 63 is said to have been caused by poison, administered by a jealous husband.

It is worth while to climb even higher up the hill – as high, in fact, as the entrance to the prison – and to follow the road that encircles the pinnacle upon which this prison is built. From this road there is a beautiful view of the lower slopes of Monteluco, on the farther side of a deep ravine, across which there is a spectacular aqueduct, flanked by a rather alarming footpath. This aqueduct, known as the *Ponte delle Torri* (Bridge of Towers) was built in the fourteenth century, but it probably reinforced or replaced a bridge built by one of the Dukes of Spoleto some seven centuries previously. It is 230 metres long, 76 metres high, and the bases of the 10 tall arches which support it are 10 metres by 12. In these days of immense bridges, these figures may not sound impressive; the Ponte delle Torri is made impressive by the steep and wild nature of the sides of the gorge.

Fourteen kilometres of winding road lead up to Monteluco, the woods of which were sacred in Roman days. The Roman temples have gone, but there are several caves and huts in which hermits lived from the sixth century onwards. There is a Franciscan monastery near the summit and both St Francis and St Bernardino of Siena came here. A much longer excursion from Spoleto would be to Norcia (58 kilometres), the birthplace of St Benedict, founder of the first of the great religious orders, and predecessor by some seven centuries of St Francis and St Dominic.

From Spoleto, the eastern branch of the Via Flaminia stretches southwards towards Rome. Terni, reached in 28 kilometres over the Somma Pass, has ancient buildings grouped around the Piazza del Popolo, but steel works and other industrial concerns have robbed it of all charm. Sixteen difficult kilometres away to the south-east, however, is the *Cascata delle Marmore*, a waterfall 160 metres in height and one of the finest in the peninsula. Terni is said to be the birthplace of the Emperor Tacitus and perhaps also of his homonym, Tacitus the historian.

Twelve kilometres farther along the road to Rome is the picturesque and very ancient little town of Narni, on its steep hillside above the gorge of the River Nera. One arch of a great Roman bridge still stands. Narni was the birthplace of one of the most famous of the condottieri, Gattamelata, whose splendid statue by Donatello – the first equestrian statue to be cast in bronze since ancient times – is one of the proud possessions of Padua. The hill on which Narni is built forms a narrow and steep-sided promontory and the main road goes two-thirds of the way round its base. The Palazzo del Podestà, the twelfth-century cathedral and the façade of the little church of Santa Maria in Pensole are only three of the buildings that justify the climb up the hill.

One last halt might be advisable before you get involved in the outer and fast-spreading suburbs of Rome. Città Castellana is built on the ruins of Falerii Veteres, which the Romans themselves destroyed after a rebellion in the year 241. It stands on a plateau of tufa rock, scarred with deep ravines, and was at one time an important Etruscan-controlled town. There are some remains of the Etruscan walls, dwarfing those of the Middle Ages, and a large number of Etruscan tombs. The fortress was built for Pope Alexander VI by Sangallo the Elder. The cathedral has an unused portico – it was made in 1210 by Jacopo di Lorenzo, one of the Cosmati family, of which four generations of architects, sculptors and workers in mosaic beautified several churches in Rome, but very few outside that city. Between Città Castellana and Prima Porta, the main road runs alongside three sections of the original paving of the Via Flaminia. Paving that may have been laid there some 20 centuries ago.

And there we end. I have followed, very roughly, the three great roads that enabled the Romans to extend their rule and their civilisation north of the Alps, to so many peoples whose descendants now stream into Italy to pass their holidays there. They come in search of sunshine and beautiful scenery, of friendly people and agreeable wines, and also – often subconsciously – of artistic and intellectual influences that have helped to create the background of their own daily lives.

The Uffizi Gallery is one of the most important picture galleries in the world, but it is not the whole of Florence. The *Autostrada del Sole* is a magnificent and, in places, very beautiful feat of road engineering, but it is not the Italian countryside. I have tried to describe some of the less known places and events, and if I have succeeded in widening, even to a small degree, the reader's interest in Italy and his desire to enlarge his knowledge of it, I shall have succeeded. And who doesn't hope for success?

Index

Index

Siena
Lucca
Urbino
Bergamo
Verona
Vicenza